Ω

Project Omega

Eye of the Beast

James Acre

Hellgate Press

Central Point, OR

Project Omega: Eye of the Beast

Published by Hellgate Press, an imprint of PSI Research, Inc.

For information or to direct comments, questions, or suggestions regarding this book and other Hellgate Press books, contact:

Editorial Department
Hellgate Press
P.O. Box 3727
Central Point, OR 97502

(541) 479-9464 *telephone*
(541) 476-1479 *fax*
info@psi-research.com *e-mail*

Book designer: Constance C. Dickinson
Compositor: Jan O. Olsson
Cover designer: Steven Burns

Acre, James, 1948–
    Project Omega : eye of the beast / James Acre.
      p.   cm.
    ISBN 1-55571-511-7 (pbk.)
    1. Vietnamese Conflict, 1961–1975--Personal narratives, American.
2. Vietnamese Conflict, 1961–1975--Military intelligence--United States. 3. Vietnamese Conflict, 1961–1975--Regimental histories--United States. 4. Acre, James, 1948– . 5. United States. Military Assistance Command. Vietnam Studies and Observations Group--History. I. Title.
DS559.5.A37 1999
959.704'3373--dc21
                                      99-31093

Printed and bound in the United States of America
First edition 10 9 8 7 6 5 4 3 2 1

 Printed on recycled paper when available.

To the men who ran Recon for MACV-SOG, and to those who risked their lives to keep us alive, and to retrieve our bodies when our luck ran out. To the men who lived, ate, drank, smoked, partied, cursed, laughed, cried, huddled in the jungle together, took incredible risks, and fought against impossible odds. Especially to those who paid the ultimate price.

America, those men are living among you now. You may not know them, but they are scattered around the country, in every trade and profession, forever changed, able to serve and protect you with arms and their lives, forever men of SOG.

There is no merit
where there is no trial;
and till experience stamps
the mark of strength,
cowards may pass for heroes
and faith for falsehood.

AARON HILL
1685–1750

Table of Contents

Foreword

Too often war books are written by historians who ain't been there or by colonels and generals who viewed the action a safe distance from where the fighting and the dying occurred. *Project Omega* — written by a Special Forces grunt whose mission in Vietnam was to penetrate deep behind enemy lines and report what Charles was having for breakfast and, when done, where he was headed — is the real deal.

Green Beret Sergeant James Acre's story is different than most military reminiscences. He was not a lifer, but rather an idealistic teenager who quit college and joined the Army during a very bad war. Somehow, he talked his way into Special Forces which in 1968 was accepting mainly volunteers with airborne experience under their pistol belts, not first term peach-faced 11Bs who usually became rifle company cannon fodder.

Acre not only made it through the tough and demanding Special Forces training, once he reported into the 5th Special Forces Group at Nha Trang, South Vietnam, he wangled his way into one of its most elite behind-the-lines strike forces — the highly secret Special Operations Group, Command and Control South.

For one year he and his colorful combat mates played cat and mouse with the North Vietnamese deep in the jungle of South East Asia. His story is a no bullshit account which tells and shows what happens behind the lines when you are on your own and have nothing more than your wits, and skill to stay ahead of one of the most cunning enemies our country has ever fought.

It's a warts and all adventure story that born-again moralists may condemn as being "offensive" for the "debauchery" that occurs with the tea ladies of the Highlands and Saigon, the profanity, the dope smoking, the money changing, and the hell raising, but from my almost five years in Vietnam I know that's the way it was. Few real warriors were angels or choir boys and this is especially true of our Green Berets, who were already into dirty dancing and dirty tricks when John Travolta was taking baby steps. No rewriting of history can change that. I especially liked the fact that Acre didn't whitewash his story as so many hypocrites have done in their remembrances of Vietnam but chose to tell it straight hard and with spice.

I have always had the utmost respect for the Special Ops people who fought in Vietnam. They were special people who led the way at great risk and the intelligence they provided saved many Americans. Their hot skinny — frequently paid for with their lives and blood — allowed the conventional units to be at the right place at the right time with the right stuff to zap Charles before he zapped them.

CNN tried its level best to dishonor the reputation of the brave men of Special Operations Group with their 1998 false and libelous attack on SOGs operations during America's misadventure in South East Asia. Acre's beautifully written and accurate portrayal of some of the actions of that noble unit will allow the reader to see how these daring young men made accomplishing the impossible routine and to also set the record straight.

DAVID HACKWORTH

Author of *About Face* and *Hazardous Duty*

Preface

A number of great soldiers served with MACV-SOG. I was a good soldier but I was not a great soldier. The stories of the great soldiers are mostly unknown and untold. The time I spent as a young man with MACV-SOG in 1969–70 was a defining time of my life. I lived and served with a small group of men in a unit known as Recon Company, Command and Control South, risking and defying death every day. I knew at the time that something incredible was happening all around me and within me; someday I would have to tell the story.

Piecing this story together has been a life's goal for years. I struggled with the writing for years. Then I struggled to get someone to read it. It is difficult to get anyone's attention when no one knows that the unit even existed. A friend from SOG once said to me, "It's all so unbelievable; why tell anyone? They won't believe it anyway."

I was ordered to not keep a diary, and I did not, so this story is written from memory. Some elements may be out of sequence, and events which were not part of my direct experience were told to me directly by the principals or were part of the prevailing common knowledge during my tour of duty.

The mission in chapter 43 is told as I remember it with one exception, the actual POW snatch was a part of another mission of which I was not a part. The events portrayed in the attempt to capture a POW were typical of many such attempts with similar outcomes.

Babysan was lost after I was reassigned to Panama, and that is where I got the news from my friends in Nam. A book about CCS must include Babysan and his loss, and I took this liberty. I was not with them physically, but I was there in spirit when this great soldier fell.

This is my story. My story is not the most important one, but it is all I have. Take it like a looking glass and peer inside Recon Company, or, if you dare, step inside with me and be there, with some of the finest soldiers ever to wear the Green Beret. Step inside the spirit of SOG.

Our Motto
We the willing,
Led by the unknowing,
Are doing the impossible
For the ungrateful.

We have done so much
For so long
With so little,
We are now qualified
To do anything
With nothing.

In 1969, this was probably every soldier's motto in Viet Nam.

Our Song
We like it here, we like it here,
Yer fuckin A, we like it here.

We shine our boots,
We shine our brass,
We don't have time to wipe our ass.

Even though we have malaria,
We still police the area.

We like it here, we like it here,
Yer fuckin A, we like it here.

Sung to the tune of "Oh Christmas Tree," by the dozen or so of us who had been together for the past year at Ft. Bragg, North Carolina, together for the last time, while part of a mass formation at Ft. Lewis, Washington, waiting to board the buses to the airport, for the trip "across the Pond."

Acknowledgments

First I would like to express my appreciation to Colonel David Hackworth, our country's most highly decorated living soldier, for taking time out of his busy schedule to read the manuscript and grace my story with a foreword.

I want to thank my friend, artist Jody Stephenson for editing the manuscript and for her encouragement and good advice. And many thanks to my publisher, Emmett Ramey and Hellgate Press at PSI Research, Inc., for believing in the work and giving it a chance.

Special thanks to my brothers-in-arms: Ron DeCarlo (WIA), Rick Hinkel, Bill Coughlan, Jim Gasseling (KIA), Jim Morse (WIA), Kevin Watson, Hensley, Gunnison, Mike Crimmings (WIA), Robert Graham, Ken Courage, David Davidson (Babysan, KIA), Mike Burns (KIA), Reich (WIA), Eddie Helfand, Frank Opel, Nimzy, Carly, Thomas (KIA), Soto, Lancelot, SGM Matamoris, MSG DeLuca (KIA), MSG Brock (even though you named me Drippy and then Rolex), SFC Taylor, Steve Waltrip, Jerry Pretner (deceased), Frank Burkhart (deceased), Johnny Strange, Ernie Masci, Weigel, Sandell, Eckrote, Crofton, Malone, Becktoldt, Bouldin, Monroe, Mini-gun Red Baron (I can't remember your name, so I've called you White), and the rest of you, whose faces I can see clearly though time has erased your names from memory. You know who you are.

Chapter 1

Kundalini

The dream seemed real. Thinking I was awake, I opened my eyes and saw a black snake coiled up on my stomach. Horrified, I screamed, leaped off the cot, and ran blindly down the barracks isle. A vicious stab of pain in my right foot awakened me when a four-by-four wooden support post in the center of the isle caught my little toe, turning it back as I ran past.

This impromptu reveille disturbed the sleep of nearly everyone in the barracks. This structure had the same familiar look as the WWII wooden barracks in which we had frozen in the winter and roasted in the summer as trainees, one large room with rows of cots and lockers. Here there was no need for windows, and the sidewalls were open to the outside, covered by screens. Most of the sleepy-eyed men I had awakened were strangers to me, several were guys with whom I'd trained back in the States. We were in this "in-transit processing unit" for several days while our records were processed.

Hopping on one foot back toward my cot, I looked around sheepishly at several curious faces, then looked outside, wondering if my outcry had been noticed by anyone else.

Mike, who had been my bunkmate back in the States, sat up sleepy-eyed on his cot, "What's the matter Ernie?"

1

"Oh, this weird dream, I dreamed there was a black snake coiled up on my chest. Damn this hurts!" I was standing in my new green boxer shorts with my foot propped on an olive drab foot locker, watching the reddened toe swell. "That post caught my toe," I said a little louder, as an explanation to the others in the room.

I started dressing in my brand new olive drab rip-stop nylon jungle fatigues. All the other new troops were getting up. Nobody was sleeping late the first day in Nha Trang. We had arrived at a major destination. Headquarters, 5th Special Forces Group Airborne, Nha Trang, Republic of South Vietnam. Still in transit, but here we would get our individual assignments. This was the headquarters that we had all been waiting for.

After breakfast we wandered around the post for a while. For the first time in ages, no mundane details to pull or from which to try to ghost (disappear before being assigned a detail). We were the lowest ranking soldiers around. E-6s and up and officers were going their respective ways. Vietnamese appeared to be pulling the details that the lowest ranking soldiers usually got stuck with, like cleaning the barracks, laundry and KP (preparing food). But this was still garrison. Starched, pressed jungle fatigues and even spit-shined jungle boots, for God's sake! This was headquarters, too much high brass around for my liking. Besides, we all looked like a bunch of recruits again and I wanted out of garrison and into the field. I looked at Mike beside me and studied his beret with the new 5th flash (patch) sewn on it. We liked the term flash, it held a special meaning for us, it had a flair about it, it sounded good. We had become something.

We were walking around the place like we belonged. The beret felt good on my head. I liked the feel of wool. I knew I'd keep that beret forever. Someday I'd hang it on the wall at home next in line with the collection of hats I'd had since I was a boy. The little beanie that said Ernie, my first real hat at two years old, the cub scout and boy scout hats, the straw hat I wore at Philmont Scout Ranch at age thirteen. Philmont was my first real experience with the outdoors that demanded something and left me hungry for more. Finally, the green beret would hang up with them.

We walked over to the area that was an outdoor museum, following the gravel paths that connected the various displays, stopping at a roofed enclosure that contained a scale model of an A Team camp.

Mike looked at me, "Do you want to go to an A Team or are you going to volunteer for C&C?"

I studied the model, "I don't know, I want both." The model showed the standard configuration, inner perimeter, outer perimeter, twelve men, cross trained in two disciplines each, prepared to train indigenous forces in counterinsurgency warfare. Then I thought about C&C, about which I knew very little, just grapevine talk. Top Secret recon missions into what the enemy considered safe territory.

One attraction was the word that C&C recon didn't get fucked with, by anybody. You could be an E-4 or E-5, and officers and even generals wouldn't fuck with you, cause you were C&C recon.

"Well, I've come this far, I'm going for C&C," Mike mused as we stared at the model.

We wandered on down the path, stopping in front of a captured .51 caliber machine gun.

"Anyway," Mike continued, "the grapevine says they want us O&I (Operations and Intelligence) people to go to C&C recon."

We had seen a C&C man at the airport at Cam Rahn Bay, while waiting for our flight to make the short hop to Nha Trang. He had his rucksack sitting beside him, and had the C&C patch on his breast. The patch was a tiger's head with a parachute above it, against a red background. I had been awe struck. He was sitting there looking experienced and in another dimension, invincible. His CAR-15 was lying across the ruck, its muzzle covered with green tape. This was the first time any of us had seen a CAR-15 (The shortened version of the M-16 rifle, which had a shorter barrel and a collapsible, sliding stock. It had acquired such a mystique that it had become an object of mythical proportions). He sat dozing, waiting for his flight, while we all basked in the mystical aura of an experienced combat soldier, and tried to not be conspicuous. He exuded an intensity I'd never seen before.

Several large painted signs were posted throughout the museum. Mike and I drifted over to one that was lettered over the shape of a gigantic beret. It said, "The essence of courage is not that your heart should not quake, but that no one should know that it does."

That night we went to the enlisted men's club. It was a dimly lit shack, with a roughly scrawled sign that said "Playboy Club" wired to nails above the door. We had our first experience with the slot machines, using the slugs that we bought with our first military payment certificates. Everyone was intrigued by the slender Vietnamese women working there and everybody was wondering the same thing. We were all nervous and horny. We were greenhorns. Our grandiose status traveling across the States on leave had ended. We were caught in the middle between two worlds. The past had not quite begun to fade, so that we could miss it, the new existence had not quite begun to set in. So we sat in the bar and felt awkward and got drunk. On the way out I stumbled and fell into the concertina wire and got firmly stuck in the barbs. Lying on my back in the middle of the coils of barbed wire, every attempt to free myself merely served to make the entanglement worse.

The stuporous faces of my friends Jim, Bill, and Mike appeared above me in a semi-circle.

"Damn, that stuff really works huh?" said Bill. Feigning more curiosity he put his hands on his knees and bent over me, examining the barbed wire more closely. His bulging forearms tightened against the rolled up sleeves of his jungle blouse, threatening to burst the seams. He was a powerful man and I was usually glad that he was my friend.

"See if you can get out," said Mike, his always mischievous smile even more wicked because of my predicament. Like me, he wasn't a big man, but he was strong and wiry, and depended on his wits.

"What the fuck are you talking about? See if you can get out my ass! Look at this tangled shit! Get me out of here you comatose ass holes!" I yelled.

"Look at the way he's talkin to his friends!" Jim said accusingly, shaking his head in mock dismay. Jim was half a head taller than Bill, nearly as power-fully built and could have stared down a Cape buffalo.

"OK," I relented, "please, ple-e-eze, will you guys get these barbs out of my body and get me on my feet."

They squatted beside me and started pulling the barbs back.

"Damn, there's one in my wrist!"

Then they lifted me carefully up out of the stuff.

"Wait, there's still one stuck in my side, OK, I got it."

We all stumbled back to the barracks while I wiped the blood from my cuts and punctures.

"Lucky for you we just had all those shots."

"Yeah, glad we got tetanus shots, my ass still hurts from that gamma gob-ulin or whatever it was."

"Some recon man you'll be, fall down in the fuckin concertina."

The night was hot and the bed sheets stuck to my body. Mortars pounded constantly outside the perimeter. The barracks was rhythmically bathed in the eerie yellow light of illumination rounds. Distant thumps and cracks and vibra-tions ejected from the darkness sifted through the screens. So many unknowns sensed but not defined mingled with my thoughts and apprehension and anticipa-tion. The contradictory nature of these feelings set my psyche on the edge of a huge void, like looking into the night sky and trying to contemplate the end of the universe. I lay in bed awake, half drunk from the drinking and half drunk from the space in which I found myself.

The next day I went to the medic. He confirmed what some other guys had already told me. "Not much to be done for a broken little toe. You'll just have to live with it till it gets better. I can tape them together for you." So he taped the toes together and I went on my way.

We also were allowed to go downtown for a while. Bicycles everywhere and cone hats and strange looking skinny women wearing black silk pants and white blouses. Old pock-marked French buildings and run down shacks shingled with flattened out coke cans. Shacks everywhere. It wasn't actually downtown. Going off post anywhere in the city was going "downtown." The massage parlor was just a few blocks from the gate. A dozen or so of the guys I knew were standing in line outside the entrance. That was something I was used to, so I stood in line with them.

The line ended inside the building at a steam bath. I undressed, hung my fatigues on a hook, wrapped a white towel around my waist, and stepped through the swirls of white steam pouring out the door of the steam room.

"Hey Acre!" came a familiar voice.

Slowly my eyes could make out the naked, towel wrapped figures of Jim and Bill sitting on the wooden bench, grinning at me like a pair of Cheshire cats.

"After last night, this is just what you need," said Bill.

"Man, this stuff is hot," I said, feeling the moist vapor penetrating my lungs.

"It's good and good for you," said Jim.

Soon my body was as drenched as theirs. The rivulets of moisture ran down our faces and bodies to the floor.

We sat in the hot fog of the steam room and laughed and sweated.

One by one we were escorted to little partitioned-off cells, in which there were cots. We were instructed by a young Vietnamese man in sign language and a few English words to lie down. Then he gave a terrific pounding of the muscles of the back, massaged arms and legs and even toes and fingers. It felt good. After this complete muscle toning, he asked in a whisper, "You want girl?" I shrugged my shoulders and nodded. He left and in a couple of minutes a woman in her twenties came in.

"Fiehundre pee," she said, shutting the flimsy door behind her. I reached for my pants, took a 500 piaster note from my wallet and handed it to her. She hurriedly stuffed the note in a purse, set it on a small table at the foot of the cot, opened the towel around my waist, and squirted some hand lotion onto my already stiffening member. Then she mechanically jerked me off. Afterwards she cleaned me up carefully with a wet cloth and left the room.

I dressed quickly, embarrassed, and found the truck outside.

On the way back nobody said much, but we laughed a lot. We had to be back in the compound at 1500 hours for paperwork.

— ◄►◄ —

An E-7 SFC (Sergeant First Class) was doing the talking.

"Anyone who wants to volunteer for C&C will so state on your cards."

I studied the Combat Infantryman's Badge stitched to his fatigue blouse, a rifle encircled by a wreath. The CIB meant he had seen combat, it was sewn on his left breast along with his paratrooper's wings. I looked down at the bare chest of my new jungle fatigues.

"If C&C doesn't sound like your cup of tea, you will be assigned to an A-Team or B-Team or to a Mike Force."

I wrote C&C on the card.

Nearly all of us volunteered. Four or five did not. The next day, our fourth at Nha Trang, the orders came down. At the top, 5th Special Forces, Airborne. Below, our assignments were listed.

Acre Sp.4 Special Operations Augmentation (CCS) MACV-SOG 5th Special Forces Airborne.

I was going. The big time. The highest level, most secretive, sneak and peek operation in the war. Studies and Observations Group. The subject of grapevine talk at Ft. Bragg, North Carolina, where we were trained. Mysterious and otherworldly. The infinite. The cadre at training didn't even talk about it, except indirectly. The job in which you could be an E-4 or E-5 and majors and colonels and even generals didn't fuck with you. None of us were scrambling for supply jobs and clerks jobs. We wanted to be in the field where they didn't fuck with you.

Chapter 2

Blackbird Good-bye
Hello

A casual acting E-5 buck sergeant strolled into the barracks and told us to get our gear together. The blackbird would be here any minute. Anticipation gathered in my stomach and surged through my body. "The blackbird would be here any minute!"

We loaded in a three quarter ton truck and the E-5 drove us to the airfield. In a few minutes a dot appeared in the sky and gradually grew into a C-130 military transport, its four propellers distinguishing it from a C-123, which was smaller and had two props. No one said a word. The plane settled onto the runway with screeching of tires and roaring of engines. It taxied to the end, turned around and came back toward us. It was painted in black camouflage instead of the usual olive drab tones. The word was that it was loaded with all kinds of special electronics gear for all kinds of special applications and secret missions. It was a distinctive mark of MACV-SOG and it was stunning.

The engines slowed a bit and the plane came to a halt in front of where we stood, then the door in the back lowered to the runway, and the crew chief waved for us to come aboard. We ran through the blast of wind and noise toward the back of the plane, up the ramp and into this dark and mysterious thing called a blackbird.

The C-130 and the C-123 were the workhorses of the Vietnam war. They were everywhere, transporting troops and supplies and armaments. A few of these were blackbirds. They may as well have had a skull and crossbones painted on their sides. There was talk of secret flights deep into enemy territory, top secret missions shrouded in mystery.

Nha Trang was on the coast, just north of Cam Ranh Bay. Ban Me Thuot was in the central highlands, north and west of Nha Trang.

Through a small porthole window I could see the jungle roll by far below. The bomb-cratered jungle. In places it was intensely green, with streams and rivers snaking their way through, cutting back and forth like switchbacks on mountain roads. Then would come areas that were defoliated, looking brown and desolate. The area around Nha Trang reminded one of the surface of the moon when viewed through a telescope.

The plane droned on toward Ban Me Thuot. I watched the propellers, felt the drone of the engines permeating the interior of the aircraft. I wondered if I was the real thing, if I was as well trained as I was supposed to be. I told myself, "This is the real thing, I'm on my way to really do it. This is 'The land of the big field training exercise, with live, pop-up, shoot back targets,'" as the cadre back at Ft. Bragg had put it.

I stayed by the window, absorbing the panorama below.

— ••••• —

The air field at Ban Me Thuot was distinguished by a cinder block terminal and tower, painted pink, which struck me as strange. It certainly stood out in sharp contrast when seen from the air. The earth was reddish, like Oklahoma earth, the source of the dinginess of the pink. The terminal and tower were obviously the oldest buildings, around which had popped up military buildings and tents. It was dry season. Everything was covered with red dust; vehicles, fatigues, weapons, buildings, papers, everything. Later the monsoons would come and everything not covered with plant life would be existing in a reddish muck. Muck covered boots, reddish tinged pants, tires and wheels crusted red from travel through the sticky, red-oxide roads.

The plane came to a stop and the rear ramp was lowered. At the foot of the ramp sat a very battered, very unmilitary looking, three quarter ton truck. It was like the ancient wrecker that belongs to the local salvage man in every small town, bent and worn from so many miles over rough roads, from so many tows. But this one was olive drab beneath the layer of red grime, and instead of gin poles and winch it had a spotless minigun mounted in the back. A suntanned buck sergeant was sitting in the truck. His fatigues were faded and instead of a beret he was wearing a worn, floppy bush hat. "CCS people load up here," he yelled through the wind and dust.

With my duffel bag slung on my shoulder I nodded to Mike, who was going on to CCN at Da Nang. "Guess we won't be bunk mates for a while," I yelled through the noise and the lump in my throat.

"It's been a good year," he said, extending his hand.

"Hope they've got vinegar and oil for your salads up there," I said as we shook hands.

"No problem, I brought my own," he answered, smiling.

"We'll get together and catch up."

"Right, maybe we can get an R&R at the same time."

"Good idea, see you soon." I trotted down the ramp toward the waiting truck.

The CCS compound was a couple of miles from the airport, and nearly ten miles from the city of Ban Me Thuot. The truck stopped at the gate, which was fortified with armed guards. A sign outside said, "Restricted Area, Stop." Our driver waved to one of the guards and he signaled for us to pass on through.

The driver stopped the truck in front of the headquarters building, which was called the TOC, for Tactical Operations Center. He told us to wait a minute, jumped out and went inside. We bunched around the truck and meandered around a little. We felt green. We had finished our training at Ft. Bragg and had sewn our 5th flashes on our berets. We were old timers there and had enjoyed our brief superiority over the new recruits, and the trainees who still had no flashes on their berets. Suddenly we were new again. Starting at the bottom again.

Standing in front of the TOC, one could see that the CCS compound was small. It was about a quarter mile long by a little less in width. Surrounding the compound was a thick maze of barbed wire and concertina wire. Beyond that, several hundred meters had been cleared for a field of fire. Wooden towers were in all four corners, and several more were spaced equally along the outside perimeters. Sand bag bunkers and an earth berm were built up around the perimeter between the towers. Permanent buildings had been erected inside the compound. Across the road from the TOC was the club. Beside the club the mess hall. Behind and beside the mess hall were the attached units. These were conventionally trained people such as helicopter personnel, clerks, typists, and mechanics, who were attached to the unit. They were allowed to wear a beret, but without a flash sewn on. The dispensary was located near the center of the compound. Special Forces medics were intensely trained to carry out all sorts of medical tasks, like keeping the wounded alive until they could be taken to a hospital, minor surgery, and keeping the girls downtown clean. They dispensed drugs and tended to the general health of the compound. Mortar and platoon companies were on the north side of the compound. Recon company was on the far east side, south of the chopper pads, near the east perimeter and the ammo dump. Recon company was separated from the rest of the compound by an invisible barrier that we would soon begin to see.

The driver came out the door of the TOC. "You guys can go over to the club till 1300 hours. Then you're to report to the TOC for a briefing," he said in a matter of fact tone. He outranked all of us by one stripe, and by the wide gulf of time-in-country.

"What do you do here?" Bill asked. He was from Chicago and not to be intimidated.

"I run recon," answered the driver, "right now I'm on stand-down."

"What's stand-down?" somebody asked.

"That's a break between missions," answered the buck sergeant, as he climbed into the truck. The engine roared and he drove toward recon company.

We stood watching the truck recede.

"Stand-down?" I said half to myself.

"You know," Rick chuckled, "that's the most beat-up truck I've ever seen." Rick was an amiable person, about six feet two, and wiry. His blonde hair coiled in tiny natural pin curls when it was longer. He never got angry, or wouldn't ever show it if he did. It kept him out of trouble. "Did you see that minigun?"

"Did I see that minigun!" We all drifted across the street to check out the club. It was a barn-like building, wide open inside, with a bar along the north wall. We took stools at the bar and ordered our first drinks. Prominently displayed on the wall behind the bar was a sign that said, "You Have Never Lived Until You Have Almost Died. For Those Who Fight For It, Life Has A Flavor The Protected Will Never Know."

I looked at my watch. 1230 hours. Bill and Jim were laughing about the trip from Ft. Bragg to Chicago. Jim and I had ridden with Bill to Chicago, then flown on home. Jim was a big bruiser with a high pitched voice. He liked to tease his friends, but he could always be counted on in a fight.

"You shoulda seen Acre when he opened his eyes and looked out the side window straight down the highway," Jim cackled, smirking over the top of his drink.

Bill chimed in, "That look on your face was worth a thousand bucks."

"I just didn't want to die before I even got here," I answered.

They were referring to the car sliding sideways in the middle of the icy bridge we were crossing. I was asleep and opened my eyes just as the car was skidding crossways down the highway, the view through my side glass the one that should have been through the windshield. Bill whipped the car back into line again and I was wide awake.

"I wrecked that car," Bill said.

"I'm glad I went on home then," I said. "What happened?"

He curled one side of his lip and said "Eh," disgustedly. "I was coming home on the freeway and a fifth of scotch fell on the floor." He started laughing. "I reached down to pick it up and when I raised up, a telephone pole was in the center of the VW."

Everybody guffawed.

＊＊＊

"A-ten-shun!"

We rose to our feet and stood at attention.

"At ease, be seated," said a major as he entered the room. He stood in the front of the room and surveyed us momentarily.

"Welcome gentlemen, to Command and Control South. My name is Major Smith. It is my duty to inform you that everything you do here is classified top secret. You are not at liberty to discuss it with anyone outside the unit. You are not at liberty to write home about this operation, nor are you to keep a diary about your assignment here. Anyone violating these conditions is subject to prosecution under the UCMJ (Uniform Code of Military Justice). Recently one man kept a diary of his assignment here and was immediately busted and shipped out. As far as the war is concerned and the people stateside are concerned, this unit does not exist. Yes, you heard correctly. This unit does not exist."

He turned to the wall and removed a drape, revealing a large map. "This is a map of North and South Vietnam, Cambodia, and Laos. Command and Control North is situated near Da Nang. Command and Control Central is near Kontum." He showed their locations with a wooden swagger stick.

"Command and Control South is here, at Ban Me Thuot. The mission of CCS, and our sister units, is to provide intelligence information on enemy troop movements and build-ups in the neutral countries of Cambodia and Laos. This information is gathered by the insertion of reconnaissance teams into denied areas. You will be required to wear sterile fatigues, that is, fatigues with no marking indicating association with U.S. military forces. I must point out to you the sensitive nature of these operations. NVA troops use these sanctuaries to assemble and supply, and the logistics operation for the insurgency in South Vietnam is carried out along these borders. Cambodia is a neutral country, but in order to maintain their neutrality they must allow the NVA to use these border areas. Cambodia cannot resist in any event. North Vietnam violates the Geneva Convention and uses territory of a neutral country to invade South Vietnam. Intelligence information from these areas is vital to the conduct of the war."

He stopped talking and walked around the front of the room, watching us. After a long silence he spoke, "Gentlemen, you've all heard of the Ho Chi Minh Trail. Now, you will join the very few who have seen it with their own eyes. Your After Action Reports will be on President Nixon's desk every morning."

He returned to the map. "CCS area of operations extends north to Duc Lap, which is the southern-most AO (Area of Operations) of CCC, and south to Bu Dop, just above the Fish Hook. The Parrot's Beak is this area of Cambodia, which juts into South Vietnam, near Saigon. We no longer insert teams into the Parrot's Beak, or the Fish Hook, here, because of the high loss of men and equipment in these areas during the last year. These are considered enemy strongholds. Other methods of gathering intelligence about them are now being employed.

"Information will be disseminated strictly on a need to know basis. You have been assigned to either recon company or to one of the platoons. The mission of recon company is to run the missions I've described, and to provide listening posts for the base camp.

"The mission of the platoon companies is to provide local security in the area of CCS and to provide bright-light teams. These are teams that are inserted to aid recon teams that are in contact with the enemy, and to retrieve bodies."

He paused. "In the event," he paused again, "In the event you are captured or killed in the areas I have described, the United States Government will deny all knowledge of and responsibility for you."

"Here are your assignments, you will receive further briefing and team assignments from your company commander. Acre, recon company, Coughlan, recon; Gasseling, A company; Hinkel, recon; Helfand, recon; Morse, recon . . . ."

I felt a pang of anticipation, then relief. Recon was where I wanted to go. I looked at the map, and the drawing of the Trail, running parallel to the border, branching off in all directions.

The officer finished reading the assignments. "Are there any questions?" He nodded to Jim, who had his hand up.

"Sir, I would like to be assigned to recon company," Jim said.

"Your present assignment is it for now. You will have to try to transfer later."

Jim was upset about this and protested, but the officer held firm.

Chapter 3

FNG

The cluster of buildings was marked only by a small sign that said, "Hdqtrs Recon Co." We newcomers waited with our duffel bags in front of the headquarters building. It was a relief to finally be away from garrison military. This place looked as though there was a mission, a real mission. It was clean, as clean as hard packed red dirt can be, and the lusterless buildings were in order, but the place was obviously one of the strictest utility. There was something else going on besides keeping the place cleaned and swept.

After a few minutes the battered screen door opened and out stepped a big Mexican man whose fatigues boasted sergeant major's stripes (the chevron with three stripes up and three stripes down, with a star in the center). The banter stopped immediately and we all fell silent. The sergeant major stood in front of us, silently surveying us with his eyes slightly squinted. He was the kind of man whose demeanor instilled instant respect, regardless of all the stripes. He boasted a full mustache, which indicated an independence, but it was a carefully tended handlebar that curved upward and did not go below the edge of his lip, so that it did not violate Army regulations. When he finally spoke it was with the authority of experience. His voice did not betray the nervous edge of younger officers, nor was it inflated by the self-satisfaction of power, qualities that were picked up immediately by younger soldiers. Here was a man not to be crossed.

"Welcome to recon, gentlemen," he said, finally. "I am Sergeant Major Matamoris." He studied the clip board in his hands and started calling roll. After each name he called was answered, he raised his eyes from the clip board and looked carefully at the person.

"Your commanding officer here at recon company is Captain Collins. He has a few words to say to you. A-ten-shun!"

The formation came to attention and the screen door slammed. A young captain about the same age as myself stepped in front of us. His jungle fatigues were tailored so that the pants were not baggy, as many young officers wore their fatigues.

"At ease," he said. "Welcome to recon company. My name is Captain Collins, commander of recon company. Each of you will be assigned to a team in the next few days, your assignments will be posted on the bulletin board inside. You will be assigned to a team with an experienced one-zero, which is the designation for a team leader, from whom you will learn first hand the mission of C and C. Before running any missions you will be sent to CCC at Kontum for in-country training."

He turned to the sergeant major. "That's all sergeant major." The sergeant major called attention, saluted, and the captain turned and disappeared through the screen door.

"These are your barracks assignments." The sergeant major read another list of our names with a room assignment next to each. "If you want to change rooms later come over here and tell me, so I'll know where everybody is. OK, take your gear over to the barracks and get settled. None of you leave the post until further notice." He turned and went inside the headquarters building.

I set my duffel bag on the concrete floor and took a look at the room. It was about eight feet wide and fourteen feet long. There were three barracks, each divided into four rooms of this size. Three of us were assigned to one room. We were fortunate to have a hooch with a concrete floor. There were even military bunks and gray wall lockers. Someone was obviously living there, personal effects were sitting about.

The door opened and a husky blonde guy set a rucksack into the room, then closed the door behind him. His fatigues were filthy with dirt and stained white with salt from perspiration. On his head was a black cap. On a leather thong around his neck was a big pewter peace symbol. His web gear bulged with magazines for the rifle.

I wasn't sure whether I had seen or smelled him first. The stench of unwashed time in the jungle would soon become familiar.

"How you doing?" I nodded. "Guess this is your room." I gestured towards the variety of things in the room.

"Yeah, I just got back from Kontum, one-zero school (the reconnaissance team leaders course). You must be Acre, I'm Deak, the sergeant major said I had a new roommate." He untied the green scarf from around his neck and threw it on top of the rucksack. "Where you from in the World? I'm from Chicago."

"I'm from Kansas, little town in the west part of the state," I answered. My eyes were glued to the gear all over him, grenades, compass, strobe light, the weapon still slung over his shoulder, the rucksack sitting on the floor.

"Farmer, huh?" he smiled.

"No, I grew up in farming country, but in town. Anybody else live here?"

"There was," he looked away, "Davis was in here when I left for Kontum. He was KIA (Killed In Action) two days ago, I just found out. He was pretty new in country. He got back from one-zero school just as I was leaving for Kontum, got it on his first mission. Looks like the other guy moved out too."

"Oh?" I said, hesitating, "Was Davis a friend of yours?"

"No, we barely crossed paths."

"Do you know what happened?"

He shrugged his shoulders and spoke quietly, "Stray minigun round, called the guns in too close they say, freak round caught him in the back. He was carrying the radio." He walked past me and looked around the room. "Guess they got his stuff," he said, even more quietly.

He set his rifle in the corner beside the rucksack, then took off his web gear and laid it beside them. "I gotta have a shower, talk to you later, OK?"

"Sure," I said, "I gotta go over to supply now, anyway. I'll get my stuff together when I get back." I headed for the door. "See you later."

"Yeah, see you later."

⋅⋅⋅ ⊷⊱⊰⊶ ⋅⋅⋅

Recon company was a world apart, and it took time to be accepted. And you had to prove yourself. I soon learned what the term FNG stood for, and why it was used. A "fucking new guy" was an unknown quantity, one that could be dangerous to everyone else. But, this was not a situation in which one could resent such a title.

No one said that the reason Davis was killed was because he was new. The point was that most people who were killed got it on their first few missions.

I soon found that military discipline is different in a war situation, and so is military courtesy. Respect for rank is still the cement of organization, but it takes on a new framework when the army is at war. A good combat soldier does not usually make a good garrison soldier. One of the paradoxes of military service.

My new roommate turned out to be a good humored fellow, always showing a jovial mood and happy demeanor. He was helpful in acquainting me with the place.

The first day we were issued our primary weapons and given a short briefing. We were issued a CAR-15, which was an altered version of the M-16. The barrel was shortened to the length of a submachine gun and it had a sliding stock, to make firing from the hip easier. Mine was one of the first that was built. It even had "Commando" engraved on the side. The outside of the weapon was a dull rust color, exposure to the tropics had taken its toll, but the inside of the barrel and all the working parts were spotlessly clean. It was in perfect working condition. For the first time I had a weapon with me constantly and had access to all the ammunition I wanted. We were free to go to the firing range and practice all we wanted.

The CAR-15 held a fascination, it had a life of its own. This was the weapon that had an entire legend built around it back in the states. I held it in my hands, felt the power of it, thought of the recon man I'd seen at the airport. Now I had one, it was in my hands.

An experienced one-zero on stand-down drove the old three quarter ton truck with the minigun that had picked us up at the airport. All us FNG's were loaded in the back, bouncing along the rutted road toward the firing range for our first lesson in jungle warfare fighting with the CAR-15.

While we were roaring over the dirt road toward the firing range SGT Burkhart reaffirmed that only SOG and a few other snoop and poop operations were issued the CAR-15. He had brought along an AK-47, which we could opt to use, to familiarize us with it.

"What do you carry to the field?" somebody yelled to Burkhart.

"CAR-15," he answered, turning his head toward the rear of the truck. "It's lighter than the AK and you can carry more rounds. You can also control it better on full auto, you'll see."

We covered the half mile to the range in a few minutes, and the beat up old truck ground to a halt in front of a three hundred meter open area, which had a berm at the rear to stop the rounds. Everybody piled out and gathered in a semi-circle to listen.

Burkhart slung the weapon over his shoulder effortlessly, in the manner Deak had been carrying his. "This is the best way to sling your weapon, tie the strap on the front sight support and on the slot on the top of the sliding stock. You will seldom need the sights anyway, and after a little practice you'll learn to have the weapon at the ready at all times.

"Notice that I've wrapped the flash suppressor with green tape, this is merely to keep foreign material out of the barrel. Now I'm going to show you how to use the weapon for short bursts."

He turned toward the berm and inserted a magazine into the weapon. "You can always hit your target at a distance of fifty meters or more, depending on how good you get, with successive bursts of two or three rounds. And you better get good.

"Start low and work your way up, starting low is better than starting too high, cause you'll have an indication of where you're hitting." The rifle erupted in successive lightening cracks just as he had described.

"Now, see that green box down on the berm?" Burkhart pointed toward an old ammo can that was leaning against a shot-up tree stump.

Everybody acknowledged with a yeah or a nod.

Three red streaks drew a course from his hip, two of them thudded into the ammo box. This brought responses of "Jesus!" and "Wow!"

"Two out of three isn't bad at a hundred meters from the hip." Burkhart took the magazine out of the weapon, removed a round and held it up, emphasizing. "I carry a couple of magazines of tracers to help direct chopper fire. Tracers aren't too good to use all the time cause Charlie can see where the fire is coming from and return fire. But you can see from this demonstration that you can fire instinctively from the hip and hit your target. All it takes is a little practice and the realization that your life depends on it. By the time you raise the weapon to your shoulder Charlie already has you drilled. Most, if not all, of your contact with the enemy will be at close range."

Each of us in turn fired our weapons in the way he had demonstrated. After everyone had fired a magazine, he picked up the AK-47.

"This is Charlie's mainstay and the SCU will be carrying it too. It's a good reliable weapon, they say you can bury it for a year, dig it up and it will still fire.

"It fires slower than the CAR, for this reason some like it better. The only problem you have on auto is that the muzzle tends to rise and after three or four rounds you're firing over their heads if you're not careful. Some like to turn it on its side like this for automatic operation, this way you spray to the side and the pull is easier to control to the side."

He fired the AK, which had a deeper sound than the CAR. We were surprised to see that the tracers were green instead of red.

The enemy's weapon. Thus began my fascination with "the enemy," "Charlie," "Viet Cong," "NVA." The weapon Burkhart was firing was a captured enemy weapon, the green tracers spitting from its barrel were captured rounds. I wondered about the man who had carried it. What had he looked like? Was he dead? Alive? Still out there in the jungle fighting with a new AK? Most of all, what motivated a man to carry that weapon down the trails from North Vietnam to the war in South Vietnam?

Shortly after we returned to the camp, recon company became very agitated, somebody was running around yelling, "Team Hammer is coming in, they got shot out!"

Sergeant Major Matamoris yelled at a couple of guys, "Take my jeep to the club and get a case of beer and some pop, they should be here in ten minutes!"

The jeep roared off toward the club. The rest of the company was gathering at the chopper pads, milling around talking, looking to the sky above the camp.

In a few minutes some dots appeared in the distance, then the drone of the turbines and the wop, wop, wop of the blades could be heard, then the dots became distinct silhouettes of helicopters approaching.

The jeep came roaring up beside us and somebody started ripping the top off the case of beer.

Then the choppers were above us, descending slowly to the ground. The roar and wind could knock a person down. Everybody was looking upwards, straining to see through the dust, waving to the choppers, where beaming dirty faces with hands waved back. The choppers landed, the roar subsided, and six filthy, bedraggled, dangerous looking, well-armed men jumped off smiling. Their faces were grimy and the days of perspiration left white salt stain patterns in their clothes resembling tie-dyed tee-shirts. Four of them looked like North Vietnamese soldiers and two of them looked like Americans, they had several days growth of beard.

Spewing cans of beer were poked into their hands, while there was embracing and shaking hands, everyone was happy. No one had been killed or wounded on the exfiltration.

"You crazy bastards!" one of the "old guys" said, amid embraces, "you can't take on a whole company."

"Shit, they stumbled right over us," answered one of the Americans.

They had barely tasted a beer when the colonel's jeep drove up and they piled inside to head for debriefing. Debriefing before anything, food, showers, anything.

Listening to the conversation I learned that a couple of NVA soldiers who were stepping off the trail to take a leak had stumbled across the team lying in the brush beside the trail. The team wasted them, but the whole company had given chase and they'd run a long ways with the NVA in pursuit.

Chapter 4

Ban Me Thuot

The next week was spent getting our rooms together, and learning about the mission of the unit. Experienced men conducted classes in the special tactics used by small recon teams, and we learned about the variety of reactions and options open to a small patrol in hostile territory.

The basic philosophy was, "Run away to fight another day." A small unit of four to ten men didn't have the firepower to sustain enemy contact. The idea was to establish fire superiority in your immediate area, get the enemies' heads down, then run like hell, calling in support. Since the basic nature of the mission was to sneak into a place and observe, once you were observed by the enemy, or "compromised," the mission was unlikely of further success and the best thing to do was get out.

Because of the distance from friendly bases, our support consisted of helicopter gunships, and only in the daytime. At night there was no support or even radio contact. Listening to these details sent shivers down my spine. At night get into the best position possible, set out your claymores, and be quiet, cause there won't be any help.

After a class in tactics, Rick and I went over to the recon TOC and checked the bulletin board. All the team names were on the board. His name was posted under "Awl." Mine was listed under team "Sickle."

Each team had three Americans. We were each the third American on our respective teams.

We looked at the board and tried to pronounce the names of our indigenous team members, or SCU, pronounced "Sioux," the acronym for Special Commando Unit.

"Sau, Bo, Tai, Song, that's got to be a Chinese Nung team," I murmured.

"Yeah," Rick said, "Mine's a Yard team. Jeez, there's just twelve teams."

"Less than forty Americans active at any one time."

After the week of classes in tactics each of us started working with the team to which he was assigned. We put into practice what we had been taught and what the "indige" SCU team members already knew. What were known as immediate action drills were repeated again and again so that every man on the team would react instinctively in the proper way to a given threat. Thus the new team member gradually became integrated into the gestalt of the team.

Our conversation was interrupted by the sound of the old three quarter ton. "Hey! You guys want to go to town for the rest of the day?" It was Burkhart behind the wheel again.

"Sergeant major says you can go now."

We jumped into the truck without hesitation.

It was several kilometers to Ban Me Thuot. The truck bellowed out the gate, leaving a great cloud of dust in its wake. Everyone who wanted to go and had time off was in the back of the thing. The others had taken off earlier in a deuce and a half.

The jungle rolled by, our first chance to see the countryside up close. After we passed the pink airport, we swayed back and forth as the old truck followed the weaving road across the land, through open areas under cultivation. Real water buffalo were out in the fields, being tended by real Vietnamese in pointed cone hats, skinny, brown, stick men with knobby knees and callused bare feet, working close to their huge horned gray beasts.

Random bunches of thatched huts blended with the foliage as though they had grown up out of the jungle along with the plants around them.

The jungle, green green, a paradise of plants, big leaves, bigger leaves, huge leaves, three feet long, little leaves, vines wrapped around leaves, around trees. An incredible sight to a boy from the great plains, where the cottonwoods strung along the Arkansas River look magnificent standing over the flatlands.

Then came the ARVN (Army Republic of Vietnam) compound, bristling with concertina wire, looking menacing with its wide open bare field of fire, hacked out of the middle of the jungle.

Crack! A bullet ripped the air above our heads.

"What the fuck!" Everybody scrambled to the floor.

"Those fuckin ARVN's are sniping at us again," Burkhart said, his head lowered beneath the top of the steering wheel. "They think it's funny or something."

Burkhart turned his head, "Everybody going to the bar? I'm going on to the B Team compound. I'll be back in a couple of hours."

There was a unanimous "Yeah!"

As we neared the city of BMT (everybody referred to Ban Me Thuot as BMT) the traffic got heavier. A new kind of traffic, three types. Olive drab military vehicles, small 50cc Japanese motorcycles, and three wheeled vehicles called lambrettas. Lambrettas had handlebars and a seat in front for the driver, and a small pickup bed with a roof. They were used for transporting goods and for taxis.

We passed a string of palm trees beside the highway, and the truck slowed down and pulled into a drive, then stopped beside a building. Everybody jumped off.

"See you guys later," Burkhart yelled over the truck's engine. "Don't pay over eight hundred P for a short time."

What initially appeared from the outside to be one building, was, in fact, four buildings surrounded by a ten foot concrete wall. The outside was scarred as though the place had been stricken with small pox. Two pairs of buildings faced each other, with a courtyard between. One had to step through a narrow doorway in the wall to gain entrance to the courtyard, then one had access to the four buildings.

I ran my finger around and inside one of the pits in the concrete, then stepped through the door into the courtyard.

We wound up in the first bar on the left. It was a big place by Vietnamese standards, one large room with well worn wooden tables and chairs, booths with torn black vinyl, and a long bar along the side opposite the entry door. Mirrors ran the length of the wall behind the bar. Ceiling fans turned slowly.

We stepped into the din of drinking soldiers and jabbering Vietnamese women. Rick and I joined Morse and Watson at their table. We called Morse "the Grit." He was from a place called Center, Texas. This afternoon his southern drawl was even slower, and his face was turning a gradually deepening red. His face always got red when he was drinking, and his smile got even broader. He waved a wiry arm for us to sit down.

Watson was a big guy from the west coast who was always in a good humor, nothing seemed to get to him. He had a girl on his lap.

"Hey, what happened to this place, did you see how shot up it is?" I asked.

"They shot the shit out of it in Tet of '68," the Grit drawled. "The girls were telling us about it. Some VC were holed up in here shooting at the 155 compound across the road, and they mini-gunned the hell out of the place."

The 155 compound was a chopper unit across the road, which also had the local PX and a hospital. At the PX you spent MPC (Military Payment Certificates). In town on the local economy you were supposed to spend Vietnamese piasters, for which we had traded MPC back at base.

Greenbacks were strictly forbidden anywhere in Vietnam. Naturally greenbacks were in high demand.

I ordered a whiskey coke, the only drink in the house, unless you wanted warm beer poured over ice. Two more girls popped up like magic and sat beside Rick and me. A short VN sat beside me and a darker skinned Cambodian with rounder face and eyes sat beside Rick.

"Hello, I am Ling," the Viet smiled and nodded to me.

"Hi, I'm Ernie," I said, somewhat sheepishly.

"You come B-50?" she asked.

"That's right, I'm at B-50," I answered. B-50 was another name for CCS. This was the term all the girls used.

"B-50 number one," she shook her head affirmatively, "you want one more whihee coe?" (I soon discovered that a good thing was always described as "number one," a bad thing was "number ten.")

I shook my head yes.

"You buy me Saigon tea?"

"Sure." Saigon tea was exactly that, a small glass of tea, the necessary preliminary, a part of protocol, I soon discovered.

She yelled something in Vietnamese to the bartender, the only parts I understood were "whihee coe" and "Saigon tea."

By this time each of us at the table had a girl next to him. Ling was particularly attractive, with well-formed features, and her skin was clear and smooth, but her mannerisms displayed a certain lack of confidence. Her long black hair reached to her waist.

Two of the girls started talking rapidly in Vietnamese and motioning discretely at a girl sitting across the isle.

"What's the deal?" I asked.

Ling pointed to the girl across the isle, then to her own oriental nose, and said enthusiastically, "She number one. I go Saigon, same-same, go doctor, number one." She motioned toward the other girl again.

I followed her gesture to the other girl. She had a perfectly shaped Caucasian nose, which contrasted with the wider and flatter noses on most of the other girls. She had saved enough money to go to the plastic surgeon in Saigon and have her nose done like a "Round Eye," and had just gotten back from Saigon. She was obviously the object of admiration and conversation in the room. She was enjoying the attention and was sitting with another trooper trying to look very dignified.

"You like?" Ling asked, shaking her head rapidly.

I shrugged my shoulders, "It's OK."

"You say number ten?" she asked, wrinkling her brow.

"No, it's OK," I said. By this time the whiskey was taking effect, and things were getting louder.

"You want short-time?" Ling asked.

"A short time of what?" I asked. Everybody at the table laughed.

"You can go upstairs with her for a short time for eight hundred P, dumb shit," Rick said.

"I know, I know," I said. "Yeah, OK," I nodded to Ling.

"Gif me hay hunred P," she held out her open palm.

I handed her a five hundred and three one hundred piaster notes.

She went immediately and talked with the old mamason who was sitting at the end of the bar, next to the stairs. Mamason's smile was a bright reddish purple, from the betel nut she was chewing, and her teeth were painted black, a favorite cosmetic of the older Vietnamese women.

Ling turned and motioned for me to follow her up the stairs.

Watson called after me, "We've only got a couple of hours."

"He only needs five minutes," Morse drawled.

"Fuck you guys," I said, and followed her up the stairs.

We entered a small cubicle that barely held a narrow bed and a nightstand. Ling sat on the bed and took off her clothes, then lay down spread-eagled on the cot.

"Guess I don't need the chapter on foreplay," I mumbled.

"You say what?" a face asked, from somewhere above lemon breasts and smooth, nearly hairless vulva sitting placidly between light brown thighs.

I said nothing.

"No sweat GI," she said in a matter of fact tone.

"Right, no sweat," I said. Awkwardly, I took my clothes off and joined her on the cot.

After a few minutes I had success, but penetration was difficult because she was utterly dry. I kissed her, but she was unresponsive, so I laid my head beside hers on the pillow. Then I heard something crunching, rather felt something crunching. I raised my head.

She was eating an apple.

"This is ridiculous," I grumbled. I managed to finish my act and started getting dressed.

She laid the apple core on the nightstand, sat up and started dressing.

"Hey Eve, how was the apple?" I asked.

Her eyes darted. "Me Ling, no Eef, you beau coup dinky dau."

"Yeah I'm crazy all right, beau coup dinky dau."

Chapter 5

A Figment

I started to feel familiar with the camp, but I was still an FNG and knew my place. There was a lot to learn. Trial by fire was still ahead. Trial by fire was the element separating us from the rest of this little fraternity living in the middle of nowhere, ten thousand miles from "the World." When the one-zeros talked, I listened.

The sergeant major called several of us up to the TOC and told us that we were going to Kontum for one-zero school. After the school we'd run what was called a "local." A local was a mission "in country."

A guy stopped me in front of the door to my hooch and showed me a newspaper clipping. I studied it carefully, it was about Davis, whose bunk in the hooch I had taken. It was from a stateside newspaper in Davis's hometown, an article about him being KIA. The article said he had been assigned to the 1st Cavalry Airmobile, in Quan Loi, and he had been killed while running patrols near the Cambodian border. Our southern launch site was at Quan Loi, in the middle of the 1st Cavalry's camp.

"Well, 'near the Cambodian border,' they got that part right didn't they?" I finally said, handing the clipping back to him.

"They just didn't say which side of the border," he nodded his head, smiling sardonically.

"This unit doesn't even exist does it?" I said.

"Nope, none of this is even here," he said, waving his arm in an arc, "it's all a fantasy, a figment of your imagination."

He acted like it was old hat, but I was incredulous.

Inside the hooch, Rick was stashing some stuff in his wall locker. He had moved in with Deak and me.

"Hey, did you see that newspaper article about Davis?" I asked.

"Something else isn't it." Rick answered.

"It's just so strange, his people don't even know the truth."

"Part of the deal," he said, shrugging his shoulders and raising his eyebrows in a look of unconcerned resignation.

"Part of the deal," I said quietly, my eyes riveted to my CAR-15 leaning against the wall.

We went to work changing the hooch around to make room for three. We stacked up three bunks in the back, three high, then put up a makeshift wall in the middle of the hooch to make a "living room" in the front. We scrounged a cot to use as a couch for the living room, and found a couple of ammo boxes for chairs.

Rick was the tallest so he got the top bunk. Deak was in the middle and I got the bottom.

At night we would lie in bed and visit in the dark.

"Rick," I said.

"Hmm."

"Sure glad you're on top."

"Why?"

"In case a mortar round comes through the roof."

"Fuck you."

Chapter 6

One-zero and Bak Si

We went to CCC at Kontum for one-zero school. We learned that there had been war between various factions for a thousand years in this part of the world. We learned that we were fighting what was defined as a limited war. They told us that the intelligence we were gathering was crucial to the conduct of the war. We learned about psychological warfare, and some of the things that were being done to defeat Charlie mentally.

One trick, which was especially pernicious, was replacing the powder in a round of enemy ammunition with plastic explosive, called C-4. We were to drop a clip of enemy ammunition in a likely spot on a trail, where an unsuspecting NVA soldier would pick it up. One of the rounds in the clip would be filled with C-4. When this round was chambered and fired, it blew the weapon up. The same thing was done with a mortar round. The idea was to get Charlie afraid to trust his own ammunition.

Then I understood the enemy weapons I'd seen displayed as trophies in the TOC, all twisted and split and contorted.

We were also to drop transistor radios that picked up only one station, ours, and trick canteens that blew up when they were opened.

After training and drilling in the nature of SOG's mission, after tactics, escape and evasion, learning the many SOPs (Standing Operating Procedures), after being redrilled and tested, the time came for the first mission.

First came the briefing. We were going on a local. We were to observe a certain trail that was known to be used by Charlie. For this one it was all Americans. An experienced one-zero would head up the mission, the rest of us would learn from him.

I carried the radio for this one, and after several times in the field, preferred carrying it. For one thing, when enemy contact was made, the "one-one" or radio operator, effectively ran the operation from that point forward. The team leader directed the team's defensive fire on the ground, while the radio operator directed the gun ships' fire, maintained contact with the support, and helped coordinate the exfiltration. I liked having the ability to direct an arsenal with the push of a button on the handset, literally at my fingertips.

The one-zero was a guy named Tom who had a year in the field and was now working at the one-zero school. Like a lot of other guys he had extended for another six months. He was slender as a Vietnamese, though taller, with a amiable attitude, which belied a deep seriousness of spirit that was revealed when his eyes met yours.

The chopper was of WW II vintage with a piston engine and a Vietnamese pilot. That combination scared the shit out of me. Tom said not to worry about it. CCC had cover from Cobras, and A-1-E aircraft, which more than made up for not having Hueys.

The Vietnamese pilots had a crazy way of flying these things, which were called "Kingbees." They would even fly the old choppers into a tight bank so close to the ground that the rotors were perpendicular to the earth, almost touching. One tiny mistake could spell disaster. I knew a roller coaster would never do anything for me again.

We sat in the open door and watched the jungle roll by beneath. About twenty clicks (a click is 1,000 meters) from Kontum the Kingbee dropped to tree top level and raced ahead, skimming the tree tops, turning left, then right, in a zigzag fashion toward the LZ (landing zone).

Suddenly the chopper slowed and dropped into a clearing in the jungle. The six of us jumped to the ground and ran into the jungle and froze.

The roar of the engine and whop of the blades dwindled to nothing. There was silence. Absolute silence. Even the natural sounds of the jungle were silenced by the intrusion of the machine that brought us. We waited for a time. We waited and watched to see if Charlie was coming to investigate.

Nothing.

We moved slowly through the jungle toward the objective, under the direction of Tom, who had the unenviable job of watching both us and the jungle.

After moving carefully about a thousand meters, through magnificent rain forest, we came upon a small stream coursing idyllically beside a large clearing, which was cultivated.

We knew from the intelligence reports during the briefing that Charlie was in the area. Now we had confirmation that somebody was definitely there.

I was transfixed by the beauty of this land.

We sat still for two hours. Tom told us to set up security and fill a canteen, while he watched the whole procedure, then we pulled back, moved upstream back into the jungle, and crossed at a point where we could leave a minimum of signs. Our objective was still several hundred meters away.

It took another two hours to get across the stream and move to higher ground, where we could have a view of the cultivated clearing with an advantage. We found some thick, waist high, brush and sat down.

No more than thirty seconds after we were barely hidden in the tall weeds, a Vietnamese carrying an AK-47 appeared. He suspected something because his weapon was at the ready. He was about fifty meters away and was walking toward the clearing. He didn't see us.

We all stared, open-mouthed.

I heard a loud "thump thump thump" and felt a cold chill run through me. I tingled all over and could feel every hair on my body standing on end, full of electricity. The thumping was my heart. I could actually hear my own heart beating from outside my chest. I didn't know it could beat so hard. I didn't know this condition existed, this remarkable fear, this rush of adrenaline. I became something else, something from within, that I didn't know existed.

The VC continued on down the trail toward the clearing and disappeared behind the brush.

We held a short meeting to decide what to do. In barely audible whispers, more lip reading than whispering, Tom told us that now we could see how difficult it could be to see a trail, until you were right up on it. It was becoming obvious how important it was to move slowly, carefully, and silently. Charlie could have easily seen us first, a chilling thought.

We paralleled the trail a ways further, moving through a stand of tall grass, when suddenly the guy who was running point stopped and motioned for everyone to crouch on one knee.

There was either a bend, or another trail joined the first one. The point man had nearly stepped on the trail. Tom motioned to set up and cross it.

We proceeded to traverse in the manner we had been taught repeatedly, one at a time, making sure the trail was secured in both directions.

The point man had made it across and the next guy was getting ready to cross, when something happened that made me realize how important all these cautions and tactics were.

A VC came down the trail, and saw the point man ducking down across from us. He was as startled as we were. He turned and ran down the trail in the opposite direction, yelling something in Vietnamese. The unmistakable sound of an AK on full automatic opened up toward us. At the same instant the point man reached out over the trail with his grenade launcher and shot the VC in the behind with the buckshot round. Bullets cracked all around us, miniature thunderbolts splitting the air above our heads.

We all opened up in the direction of the fire, except one man fired in the other direction down the trail, while we began our retreat.

Apparently we had reached the trail just moments ahead of at least a couple of VC.

We retreated away from the point of contact, back into the brush, under some willow-like bushes. Tom told me to make radio contact and call for an exfil.

After HQ established that we were not in a firefight, not being pursued, no one was wounded, and didn't need gunship support, they decided to pull us out anyway.

Tom said the mission had to be classified as a failure. We had made enemy contact, compromised on the first day, and hadn't made it to the primary objective, which was the main trail we were supposed to observe.

I was glad, because I was so rattled, the prospect of staying out there the rest of the night was not attractive.

"Did you see that guy?" I whispered to Tom.

"No, but I've been in this area before," he whispered.

"He was young, looked like a kid with a gun."

"They're just a bunch of ragtags around here," Tom answered, still whispering, "wait till you have to deal with the NVA, your shit can get weak in a hurry."

We dropped a smoke in the clearing we had chosen for an LZ, the FAC (Forward Air Control) plane confirmed the color of the smoke, and the old King-bee settled into the elephant grass. We all piled on the chopper and the engine strained to take off. The engine wound to a fever pitch and the chopper shook like an out of balance washing machine, but the wheels remained firmly planted.

"Somebody off!" the crew chief yelled, "too much weight!"

I looked at Tom, he jumped off and motioned for me to follow.

The chopper lumbered into the air, made it above the trees, and disappeared.

"How often does that happen?" I asked.

"Whenever the conditions are wrong," he answered, "some of the choppers are stronger than others. It has to do with the weight, the temperature, humidity, and how straight up the chopper has to go."

"Glad this was just practice," I said. "I wonder if Charlie knew it was practice."

I still preferred to carry the radio.

After the exfiltration we were debriefed immediately, everything just as it would be when we returned to BMT. Then we cleaned up, and went to the club to relax.

Our conversations were exuberant, full of discussions about tactics and actions in the field.

Tom congratulated us for earning our CIBs.

"We'll get our CIBs for that?" I asked.

"Sure, it was enemy contact," he answered. "Who did you think Charlie was shooting at?"

"But it wasn't that much," I said.

"Those AK rounds sound pretty friendly to you did they?" he asked. "Don't worry, you'll hear plenty enough to feel like you've earned it before your tour is up."

I was glad I hadn't panicked and lost my head. The old timers said no one ever really knows for sure if he'll keep his wits till he's been there. I wondered about the VC who'd got it in the ass with the buckshot round. He was still out there somewhere, lying in some grass hooch, bleeding.

Next it was time to go on a mission with the team to which I was assigned. Team Sickle's one-zero was getting short, the euphemism for leaving Vietnam soon.

On the morning of our insertion we sat waiting on the chopper pad. I surveyed the team members, with whom I was barely familiar. They looked frighteningly like the Viet Cong I had seen three days before, except they were better equipped, more like the NVA regulars Tom had mentioned. They had AK-47 assault rifles, North Vietnamese fatigues, boots styled after NVA regiments. They looked enough like VC or NVA to give us a split seconds edge if our point man ran into Charlie. A split second that would make all the difference in the world.

Sau was the point man. He was younger than I. I was only twenty, he was nineteen. He had been in the field since he was fifteen, most of that as a point man. He looked barely seventeen, but for the intensity of eyes that had prematurely looked deeply into death and life.

Bo was fascinating, he knew more English than the others, except for Tai, the interpreter. Bo had a genial, expressive disposition and had promised to take me to Da Lat someday, where there were "number one girls, number one city."

Song was the fourth SCU going on this one. He was the oldest one of the group, with the strong body and square shoulders of a mature man. He was obviously the most experienced soldier among them and was the leader. He was always laughing and joking with Bo. When a dispute arose, Song was the one who inevitably settled it with firm words and keen looks.

The American team leader I didn't know, had never met before being assigned to the team. His name was Mac. He was about five-ten and red headed. He'd just come back from Bangkok.

The rest of the team was staying behind. The other American on the team was on R and R.

The fifth SCU was Thong. He was really a kid. He claimed he was eighteen but looked fifteen or sixteen. The other SCU seemed to take care of him and try to keep him out of the field, preferring for him to stay behind and take care of the barracks and their belongings.

Only one member of the SCU really made me nervous. That was the one who had been AWOL (absent without leave) when we left BMT. He was a slovenly, evil appearing character, with a scar across the right side of his face. His narrow eyes were wicked looking, his face always a mask of deception. I didn't want to go to the field with him. Apparently the SCU didn't either, because they always managed for him never to go, and he eventually disappeared, which led to speculation that he was a VC informer.

The morning was beautiful. It was calm and cool at sunrise. Even the usually active and noisy camp was somehow sleepy and groggy on this morning. It stood in distinct contrast to my emotions.

The anticipation was slowly building, as though my brain was slowly boosting the adrenaline level in my bloodstream, the new found presence of the previous day was awakening once again.

I thought about the news we'd gotten. Jenkins, a member of our group that had come in country together, was KIA up north at CCN. They'd made contact and were in the middle of an exfiltration. Charlie gave him a bullet in the back of the head while he was running to the chopper. I hoped the crew chief or door gunner was on the ball when I ran to the chopper. Could have happened to anybody.

The SCU were visiting quietly in Chinese, the tone of their voices rising and falling in gentle waves that swept past my ears in an unfamiliar current.

Then the choppers were on the pad, Hueys this time, and we were on board and aloft, the silence of the wait shattered by the whine of the turbines and the slap of the blades in the air.

Silence again. The total, immeasurable silence. The Chinese moved like cats. We wound our way through, zigzagging around clearings full of elephant grass. Each blade of elephant grass was an inch wide, six feet and taller in places. It made me feel small, as though I'd shrunk to a height of two inches. I made the novice's mistake of running my hand down a blade of the grass. It cut deeply into my finger, which bled profusely. It hurt like a paper cut.

Move a few steps and wait, looking, looking, trying to penetrate the dense growth with our eyes. When a man was low and stationary he was nearly impossible to see, even when he was very close. Movement could be seen. We had to see them first.

Ambush was the fear. All six of us could be lying dead in five seconds. The FAC plane wouldn't be able to get us on the radio, they'd send in a bright light team and find us all lying dead in our tracks. Thoughts like this flickered occasionally, a stimulation of awareness. It kept me alert.

Around mid day we stopped to eat. The Chinese sat in a circle around the team leader and me, facing out in all directions. The team leader and I studied the map, figuring how far we'd traveled, finding our approximate location.

The terrain was not very distinctive. There were no good landmarks on which to get a fix.

A barely audible voice spoke into my ear from the handset hung on my web gear (I had the volume turned way down). "Sickle this is Black Spoke, how do you read me?"

I clasped the handset and whispered into it, "Black Spoke, this is Sickle, I read you lima charlie (loud and clear)."

"Roger, we have a team in contact, advise stay in position until exfil is complete."

"Roger, this is Sickle, out," I answered.

"There's a team in contact," I whispered to Mac, "they want us to sit tight."

He looked hard at me, then poured water into the freeze dried packet of LRP (Long Range Patrol) rations. "Wonder who it is," he whispered.

I shrugged my shoulders and shook my head and took a bite of chicken and rice.

We sat in the same spot for several hours, waiting for the FAC to come back into our area.

Sitting still was fairly safe, if Charlie didn't have you spotted. He'd have to be moving to find you, and chances were you'd see him first. Mac and I studied the map of the target area and the trail we were to watch.

The FAC came back later in the day and told us to proceed. We managed to move another thousand meters closer to the target, with no sign of Charlie. By six o'clock it was time to find a place to hide for the night. We found the most dense jungle in the area and sat down again.

I heard voices on the radio and quickly put the headset to my ear. One of the conventional units had a LRP team on a recon and they were requesting an exfiltration. By sheer coincidence we had been assigned the same frequency that day. I started smiling and choked a laugh.

Mac looked at me quizzically. "What's so funny?" he whispered.

"Some LRP team wants an exfil, cause some guy has a leach on his dick," I answered.

"A leach on his dick?"

I could hear only the FAC plane's side of the conversation, but finally managed to sort out what was happening. "They've been talking back and forth about it," I said, "The guy doesn't have a leach on his dick, he has a leach in his dick. Apparently a leach crawled up his dong."

"Oh Christ!" Mac grabbed his stomach and choked his laughter.

We sat there in the middle of hostile territory, with tears streaming down our faces, like some ludicrous silent movie with no captions.

The LRP team finally got their exfil and we got ready for the night's wait. When twilight was nearly gone we quietly moved to a place a few meters from our original spot, put four claymores out around us, and huddled together for the night.

The darkness was total. The night sounds of the jungle would have been soothing if not for the electricity that coursed through my bloodstream, keeping the night sleepless.

Morning's light came slowly, the blackness giving way magically, first to indistinct shapes and forms, then to living rain forest.

Shortly after sunrise the FAC came on the radio. We confirmed our continued existence and our location and headed for the trail we were to observe.

Before eleven in the morning we stumbled across the trail. It was wide enough for two men to pass and was well used. We came across it in a bad spot.

Having just crept across fifty meters of tall grass with poor cover, we were getting ready to fade on into the brush, when the trail appeared, skirting the brush beside the clearing behind us. We hesitated momentarily, deciding what to do. We didn't want to cross the trail, for fear of leaving signs, and we couldn't watch it from the location we were in. But there was no time for decisions. A squad of VC came down the trail and opened up on us a split second after we opened up on them. The split second was enough. We fell back and to the side and got into what little cover we could find. I got on the radio immediately, informing the FAC that we were in enemy contact. The exchange of fire lasted a couple of minutes. Then there was a lull.

A piercing scream tore through the jungle and reverberated inside my head. "Bak si! Bak si! Bak siiiiiiii!" He was screaming "doctor" in Vietnamese.

I felt sick.

All was still, but for the screaming of the wounded man. We listened to him for several long minutes.

"Lets go in after him," Mac said.

I didn't answer.

"Stay behind and give me cover," he said.

We headed toward the sound of the voice.

"Stay here and cover us, stay on the radio," he said, pointing to a knoll of earth.

Sau and Mac went on into the fire. When I opened up beside them as they ran ahead, somebody opened up on me and bullets ripped in my direction, tearing through vegetation and smacking into tree trunks. I heard my first bullet to crack past my head. The bullet so many teachers had told me about. The bullet that cracks over your shoulder so close by your ear it leaves you deaf on that side for an hour, and tells you something about life and death.

They came back in a couple of minutes eternity and we ran back across the clearing to the rest of the team.

Then the choppers were over us and we got in a defensive posture as close together as practical and dropped a smoke.

"I have dropped smoke!" I yelled over the gunfire.

"I see blue smoke," the FAC answered.

"That's a Roger," I answered, "We need support fire fifty meters sixty degrees."

"Roger, confirm fifty meters, sixty degrees."

"Roger," I answered.

All hell broke loose in a chaos of noise, the volume so immense that it was total, as the gunships zoomed over raining down death in the form of rockets and miniguns. After two passes we weren't taking any fire. There was no sound in the direction of the enemy. The gunships made two more passes, then all four came by at once, unleashing holy terror, while the slick (the Hueys that carried men and supplies were referred to as slicks) came in to pick us up. The slick landed, bringing its whirlwind into the clearing, while the jungle exploded all around us. We piled onto the chopper, it was up, and we were gone.

"What did you find in there?" I yelled over the sound of the turbine.

"I shot two of them when I got in there, then got back out. No time to pick anything up, too much fire," he yelled.

"What about the guy who was screaming?" I screamed.

"I put him out of his misery, shot him in the head." He smiled grimly.

"Aren't you getting short?"

"Three weeks," his lips said.

I stared out the chopper door at the vista below.

Above the sound of the chopper blades, and the turbine whining, and the guys yelling to each other, an agonizing, piercing, tortured scream echoed inside my brain, "Bak si! Bak siiiiiiiii!"

And I heard that bullet cracking past my skull.

Chapter 7

Rats

The training at CCC in Kontum was over. We had gotten our OJT (on the job training). Although the missions were unfortunate in the sense that we had made enemy contact, and had to be considered unsuccessful, I had some experience in dealing with combat, performing under fire against the enemy. I had learned the importance of the elements that give a small recon team the edge, the edge that it must have in order to survive. And the reason for the ominous forewarning to absolutely never walk trails, no matter how rough the going, had become crystal clear.

The fear was the main thing. The fear that made one's heart beat so hard and fast that one thought it would surely burst. The fear, and the anticipation of that fear. The chaos of a firefight, the chaos of the soul, both of which had to be contained, controlled, used.

The coincidences of both these training missions were remarkable. Both times we had been extremely lucky. We had seen them first. Thinking about it too long was unnerving. Being aware of it was necessary, it could keep me alive.

Maybe that's why we drank so much in the evenings back in relative safety, in the security of the base camp, surrounded by friendlies. The night before going back to Ban Me Thuot we drank a lot. Drinks were a quarter apiece and we spent a lot of quarters.

Just outside the back door of the club was a mortar pit. A hole about four feet deep and six feet in diameter was dug, in which was placed an 81mm mortar. This was one way of making a semi-permanent mortar installation safe from incoming shrapnel. It wasn't safe for drunken soldiers just out of the field, however, and Watson stepped outside the back door to take a leak, and fell in the pit. He landed on top of the mortar and the thing caught him straight in the face, making a round cut around his mouth and knocking out his top front teeth. He caught hell for that and was the butt of many jokes while he was waiting for partial dentures.

"Sure Watson, some recon man, can't even find your way outside the club to take a piss without taking a bite out of a mortar tube."

He was a good sport and took the gibing. After all, he was the guy who was sneaking up to a trail, and ran head-on into an NVA soldier creeping directly toward him. They saw each other at exactly the same time, about twenty meters apart. Both froze in their tracks, stood looking at one another, eyes locked for deadly seconds, then slowly stepped backward, weapons trained on each other. Both had the presence of mind not to fire, because the other could have fired at the same instant, and both would have died.

It was good to be back in Ban Me Thuot. Rick and Deak and I decided to paint the front room bright red. Actually, a can of red paint is all we could come up with, unless we wanted olive drab, and Rick and I painted it red while Deak was in the field. Then we got some little jars of paint and began the meticulous job of painting psychedelic flowers and designs on the red walls.

We didn't have any stereo equipment in our rooms yet, but the guy next door did. He'd managed to get hold of some at the PX. He also had two albums, *Cheap Thrills* by Janis Joplin with Big Brother and the Holding Company. It echoed through the walls for weeks.

"You know you got it, shout if it makes you feel goo-oo-oo-ood!"

The other album was the early Animals record, the one with "Sky Pilot," which we sang in the middle of the night at the top of our lungs, during the poker parties when the guys had several hundred dollars in the pot.

"Sky Pilot. How high can you fly?

You'll never, never, never, reach the sky."

Our contact with "the World," and our picture of the "revolution" happening in America was molded by letters from home, radio Saigon (the military radio station), and by whatever records we could acquire.

The next afternoon, as I was walking into the yard between hooches, I noticed Hensley lying on the ground holding a claymore detonator, with the wire stretched out, and the blasting cap stuck just beneath the wall of his hooch.

"Hensley, what the fuck are you doing?" I asked.

"Shhh!" He waved me back. "I'm going to get that bastard."

He had a piece of meat tied to the blasting cap at the end of the wire. A pair of beady eyes appeared from the darkness beneath the hooch, there was a tug on the wire. He pressed the clicker, Bap! The cap exploded.

"Got you, you son of a bitch!" He ran to the hooch and reached underneath, pulling out by the tail the lifeless body of a huge rat. He swung it in a circle and threw it into the clearing.

"All right!" A cheer went up from everybody watching.

The battle with the rats was never ending. They lived in the spaces in the walls and underneath the hooches. They seemed resistant to rodent poison, the poison disappeared but the rats multiplied. So we were forced to undertake harsh measures in order to win. I made a KIA and WIA (Wounded In Action) list and taped it to the wall in the living room. We set huge traps and when one was killed I'd put a mark under KIA. When a trap was snapped and the rat got away I'd put a mark under WIA.

The rats came out at night after we went to bed. They'd raid anything left out. They liked soap. You might reach for your bar of soap in the morning and it would be half gone. They'd fight in the middle of the night and chase each other around, chirping and screeching, sometimes even running across your sleeping body. One night I woke up and screamed, a rat was nibbling on my toe. We disdained those huge ferret-sized rats.

One time a big one was caught by the tail in one of the traps. Hensley poured insect repellent all over him and lit it, then let him loose from the trap and watched him run around burning and squeaking till he flamed out and lay there smoking.

I See Number One

Three days after returning from one-zero school, we got word that team Sickle was to prepare for insertion. We got the team together and started getting our rucksacks and weapons ready. Ready to cross the "blue line" into Cambodia. It was the middle of March.

Although rainy season was still three months away, it was raining in the morning and the afternoon. Rain was a big element against us. No support in the middle of a monsoon.

Later in the year the monsoons would come in a wall. You could be standing in one place perfectly dry and watch the wall of water beneath the clouds come toward you. It was like stepping into a waterfall. Sometimes it would stay hazy and cloudy for several days at a time in any given place. This was dangerous. The choppers would have a difficult time getting to you, even if they weren't grounded.

I laid everything out on the cot in the red front room. Deak and Rick were already in the field. This mission was for five days. I laid out food for five days, ten packages of LRP rations, culling out the ham and scalloped potatoes to give to the SCU. (The ham and scalloped potatoes were infamous.) Cans of fruit and cans of bread from C rations, one for each day. Got lucky and found two cans of pound cake, everybody's favorite. A two quart bladder canteen, and a one quart canteen, this was enough, we would be able to find water this trip. Halazone tabs, for purifying water. My pill bottle, which contained Benadryl for insect bites, green hornets, an amphetamine for fatigue and lack of sleep. Adrenaline was plenty for me, but I carried them anyway, just in case. Malaria pills, the big orange ones and the little white ones. No matches, just my lighter for the occasional cigarette. PRC 25 ("Prick 25") radio, extra battery, claymore mine, six smoke grenades, three hand grenades, two CS (tear gas) grenades, insect bottle full of CS powder (in case dogs were on our trail), insect repellent, blood expander for somebody losing blood, morphine for pain if wounded. Twenty magazines (four hundred rounds) of M-16 ammo. I carried only 400 rounds since I had the radio. WD-40 and bolt grease for the CAR-15. Mirror and orange panel. Compass. Maps of the AO (area of operations), code book, numbered items for communications of key words in case Charlie was on our radio frequency. Strobe light, for flashing at night in case, God forbid, we had to be pulled out at night. Poncho liner, to huddle under for warmth at night. Extra pair of socks.

Somebody yelled mail call. I dropped what I was doing and hurried out to the clearing by the Recon Hqs. Several of the guys were waiting for letters from their wives. I didn't have a wife. A girl I'd met not long before going into the service wrote me a few letters. She sent me a copy of the old poem "Desiderata." It was the first time I'd seen it. It reminded me to cherish my career, however insignificant, because it was a real possession in the winds of time. It also reminded me to remember what peace may be found in silence. Despite having already learned a lot about silence, I appreciated the poem and hung it on the wall, reserving the irony for myself.

She was in the university at Wichita, the president of her sorority. It was "the" sorority at the university. The women who belonged to the Tri Delts had seemed above it all somehow. I remembered how strange it had seemed to find that even the president of the sorority was human too. She'd been delighted when I suggested that we go fly a kite at night with a little flashlight attached. When it worked she laughed and laughed. We watched the faint silhouette of the kite moving lazily about, flashing the tiny light around.

I smiled and wondered what would have come of it. Then I came back to the present and focused on the things I had laid out on the cot. I put the letter in my locker and went back to work, carefully packing the rucksack.

After my gear was together, I hitched a ride into town in the afternoon and went to the PX, then hitched on to the B team compound. It was a pair of two story buildings made of huge hand hewn logs. It had been a resort in another era. People said it was the place Teddy Roosevelt stayed when he came to Vietnam to hunt tigers. Now those two buildings were the center of the B team compound. They were magnificent buildings. I went to the PX there and spent a dollar and a half for a bottle of VO. Six months later those beautiful buildings burned to the ground.

I walked back downtown and explored the shops and watched the people. An old mamason wanted me to buy some sugar cane or some eggs. I bought a loaf of French bread from another mamason and sauntered over to the steam bath for a good steam and a blow job.

Afterwards I went across the street to a place that looked like a coffee shop and asked for a dish of ice cream and a coke. The ice cream must have been a big deal. The waiter called to the back in a tone that sounded as though it were something special, then brought a small bowl containing a tiny scoop of vanilla to the table extremely carefully, as though afraid he might drop it. Then he made a second trip to bring the coke. I studied the bottle. Just like the bottle back in the States. I wondered about the possibilities of poisoning a bunch of GI's. All they'd have to do is poison a batch of Coca-Cola. Maybe Charlie liked a coke too when he came to town.

I wandered around the streets for a while. Not many Americans were walking around. Mostly military vehicles whizzed here and there. I wasn't armed. Charlie could get me now if he wanted.

An aged woman hobbled across the street, bent beneath the weight of two big pots hanging on the ends of a six foot pole lying across her shoulders. She was dressed in solid black and was brown and wrinkled as an old uncared-for leather coat. In her pots were chunks of coal. She sat on the sidewalk and waited for a customer. This old woman was intriguing because she looked so very poor and exuded hardship so strongly that I could feel it around her when I walked by. Her eyes met mine, she smiled her broken-toothed red betel nut smile, there was a magical feeling about her.

I went to the bar for a couple of drinks. The place was nearly empty.

Li, the Cambodian, came over and sat down. "Where Rick?" she asked.

"He's in the field," I said.

She smiled. Her front teeth were rimmed by a thin line of gold. "Rick go Cambodia," she said, the smile was gone.

"He's in the field," I said again, and took a drink of whiskey coke.

Ling and another girl came over and sat down. Li said something to them in Vietnamese, with the name Rick mentioned a couple of times.

"Ah, doe mam," Li said.

"What are you talking about?" I asked.

They stopped their chatter, and looked at me.

Li spoke, in halting English, "VC number ten, B-50 number one. You know, you know, Tet sixty-eight, VC come Ban Me Thuot, go hotel night time, kill all girl, kill all girl."

I looked to the other girls. They nodded their heads affirmatively.

"What happened?" I asked.

Ling answered this time. "VC come hotel, take rope, tie girls," she made a noose with her hands and tied the imaginary knot around her neck, "VC kill girls, say number ten, hang off hotel."

I imagined the horrible spectacle of young women tied and hanging from the hotel balconies. I grimaced and studied my drink.

They patted my hand and my arm. "No sweat, VC not come long time, you number one."

Chapter 9

Jungle Mimes and NVA

Kilo 36 was the designation of the target. It was several miles from the famous Fish Hook (where the legendary Sergeant Jerry Shriver was lost), a part of Cambodia which jutted into Vietnam, the border forming a fish hook shape. The Fish Hook was near the Parrot's Beak, another area of Cambodia which projected even further into Vietnam and came within forty miles of Saigon.

We were to walk in from a Special Forces A Camp called Bu Dop, which was located near the border. During the day the choppers would wait at Bu Dop. The target objective was about two miles inside Cambodia.

We left before daybreak, paralleling Highway 14 at first, then crossing a rubber plantation, then going into the undergrowth, where we came upon the first of several small streams.

After crossing one stream we sat down for a few minutes. Feeling something uncomfortable on my leg, I pulled my pants leg up and found two thick, long, leeches securely attached to the inside of my calf. I doused them with insect repellent. They eventually dropped off, leaving cross shaped incisions in the flesh. One of them didn't heal for months.

We moved back toward Highway 14 and found the wreckage of a bridge that a member of our unit had blown a couple of years before. This bridge crossed the river that formed part of the border between Cambodia and Vietnam in this area. We sat in the brush while Mac explained the way they blew the bridge. He pointed to the twisted metal support girders that had been cut in half with shaped charges, causing the bridge to collapse into the river bed. He said there used to be lots of travel across it between Cambodia and Vietnam before Charlie took over the border areas. Now the split pavement was blotched with tufts of tall grass and was nearly covered. Across the river and what was left of the bridge, the remains of the highway disappeared into the jungle.

We found a squat tree nearby, and settled beneath its foliage covered branches to wait out the night. The FAC signed off just before sunset and we were alone with the jungle.

The gradual fading of the twilight into darkness felt like doom approaching. It got so dark I couldn't see my hand in front of my face. We didn't take off our web gear for any reason whatsoever. The only time we removed our packs was to get something from them, and this we did one person at a time, immediately leaning against the pack again and hooking the straps around our arms after retrieving the necessary item. When it rained, we got wet. Ponchos were too hot, too much trouble. We huddled under our soaked poncho liners to keep warm.

The rain soon made its way through the tree and every part of my body was soaked, except my armpits and crotch. The night passed slowly in the rain.

The rain quit sometime around midnight, then the wind blew through the trees, wailing a song of loneliness and of solitude.

I formed a mental picture of the distance back to the launch sight. The choppers were gone now, back to Quan Loi. I saw myself huddled in the middle of this foreign jungle, ten thousand miles from everything I had ever known. How intensely the wind rustled the trees, how solid was my heartbeat, the blood I felt pulsing through every vein, the breath of my lungs and of the others, quiet, rhythmic, alive.

A jet passed overhead at a high altitude, I could hear its distant rumble. I visualized the man in that jet. I wanted to talk to him on the emergency radio. "Hey! We're down here and you're up there, ain't that somethin?" The emergency radio was a last ditch communication for survival. The pilot up there seemed very real and close, even if I couldn't talk to him.

Around two in the morning I heard the distant rumble of jets again. Then the jungle ahead of us in Cambodia lit up like a lightning storm, a solid barrage of thunder erupted. The sky was flashing, the ground shook beneath us. It was a B-52 strike in Cambodia, directly ahead in the direction we were to go in the morning.

"Jesus, wouldn't you love to be in the middle of an arc light?" Mac whispered.

"You bet," I whispered. "Hope they've got everything coordinated, what a bitch if they dropped them tomorrow when we're in there."

"Fuckin Charlie is awake tonight."

After first light and making radio contact with the FAC, we moved north, upstream, to find a spot to cross the river.

The interpreter tapped me on the shoulder. He whispered that the SCU were sick. Their feet were hurting and they had diarrhea. I told Mac.

"What do you make of it?" I asked.

"One of two things," he whispered, "either they're sick, or there's something big in there and they don't want to go in."

We questioned the interpreter about it and he assured us that they really were sick, that he was OK and was going on with us. He motioned and whispered to one of the SCU. He took off a boot and held up his right foot, revealing an oozing hole an inch in diameter in the ball of the foot.

Mac said to notify the FAC and have them tell us what to do.

FAC told us to pull back and get ready for replacements.

We found a clearing not far from the river. I flashed the FAC my mirror and he confirmed our position. Then I lay down in the clearing and put the orange panel on my chest.

The chopper appeared out of nowhere and set down. The SCU jumped on, and off jumped Deak! We ran into the brush with the rest of the team.

"What the hell are you doing here?" I asked. "Thought you were in the field."

"We came out yesterday. They said they needed somebody to come in, so thought I'd come along for the ride," he chuckled. He reached into his ruck and brought out orange pop for everybody.

"All right!" We soaked up the pop like manna from heaven.

"What the fuck did you guys paint the room red for? You crazy or something?" Deak asked.

I shrugged my shoulders. "We had the paint, so we painted it."

"Yeah, but bright red? Christ, I about fell over when I opened the door."

This left four of us. The interpreter to run point, Mac, Deak, and myself.

We moved back to the river and followed it north again, until we came to a huge tree lying across from bank to bank.

The interpreter went first, after we checked the area out. He got across and covered for Mac. After Mac crossed it was my turn.

In the middle of the log of course I slipped and fell, crashing into the water. I was turning head over heels in the rapidly moving current, thinking, "Well Charlie, you got me now, go ahead." But there was no Charlie, and I managed to right myself and get near the bank. Finally I got some footing in about three feet of rapidly moving water.

I looked back to my team mates, who were watching me with smiles on their faces. Streams of water were pouring out of my pockets, rifle, bush hat, rucksack.

I trudged back upstream to the log, was able to jump high enough to press myself up and get across it on my stomach, scrambled to my feet, and finished the crossing.

We went into the jungle and I poured the water out of my rucksack and made a radio check.

We tip-toed through stand upon stand of huge bamboo. Some of it was six inches in diameter. The slightest brush against it sent a loud knock through the forest, which could be heard forever.

When we got away from the river the bamboo thinned out and we saw tall trees covered with vines. There was thick undergrowth in places, in other areas the canopy above kept the undergrowth down enough that it was relatively easy to walk through. In some locations the earth was a soft carpet of mulch between huge trees, which in other circumstances I thought would have been a wonderful place to play.

We crept a few meters, stopped, moved a few more, stopped, looked, listened, listened. The closer we got to the target, the slower we moved.

Late in the morning we were sneaking through the most beautiful vegetation I had ever seen. My peripheral vision caught some motion, to the right, about thirty meters away, two VC, with AK-47s and carrying large white sacks, were moving parallel to us, walking briskly. I stopped, moved up to Mac and tapped him on the shoulder and pointed to the right. He moved up to tap the interpreter but he had seen them. We crouched on our knees for agonizing moments. We watched them disappear ahead of us. We waited to see if more would come, but none did.

Mac sent the interpreter over to where we'd seen them. He came back and confirmed Mac's suspicions, there was a trail there, paralleling our direction of travel. We moved away from the trail, and headed on.

We had seen them first, they hadn't seen us, we weren't compromised. We could go on toward the target. This was the most mysterious feeling I'd ever known. Four of us, sneaking into Charlie's back yard. If we were lucky, he wouldn't even know we had been there.

A little after noon it rained again. When it rained and the clouds had the area socked in, we tried not to move unless absolutely necessary. The choppers couldn't support us in the middle of a monsoon. The FAC wouldn't even be able to find us. It was best to stay put.

When the rain quit, it got very quiet and peaceful and clean in the shade of the canopy. The air was a pleasure to inhale.

We moved on for a few meters when the point man stopped and motioned for Mac to move up with him. There was a trail the width of a vehicle, with two deep ruts, winding its way through the undergrowth.

The stillness was shattered by a sploosh, sploosh, sploosh. Two NVA soldiers appeared with their rifles slung at their sides. We could easily have mowed them down.

We froze in our tracks. They were walking directly toward us, following a slight curve in the ruts. One of them had a big mole on his cheek. The other had black horn rimmed glasses. I was entranced. The muzzle of my CAR-15 followed them. They were no more than ten meters away.

"This is crazy," my brain said to my pounding heart. "How can you not see me, all you have to do is look this way, no, don't look this way, don't make me do it." The round was chambered, the safety was off.

They sloshed on down the trail, talking freely. After they disappeared, we fell back away from the road. Two ruts wide enough for a vehicle constituted a road. We sat down and asked the interpreter what they were talking about.

"They say, tired, very tired, build bunkers all day, go back camp, eat, hungry."

"Bunkers? Shit! Anything else?"

"No, all I hear."

Maybe that explained it. They were dead on their feet and didn't even look to the side. That and they thought they were in safe territory.

I tried to imagine myself in their situation, walking down a road. I couldn't imagine not having seen us. Maybe they saw us, but just kept their cool, would get help and come back to ambush us. But nobody came.

The enemy. I had seen the enemy up close in his own territory. It was incredible! I wrote everything I could to describe them. Not VC this time, NVA regulars from North Vietnam. Each had an AK-47, they wore Khaki fatigues, one had glasses, the other the mole. The mole, that ought to get them back at the TOC. They had no headgear, no rucksacks, no gear at all.

Carrying no gear meant they had been working someplace close, then headed back to their camp, also nearby, when they crossed our path. So the interpreter's translation made sense. We were in the middle of something.

We moved away from the trail a few more meters and bedded down for the night. During the night we heard voices and heard people moving down the trail both ways. Nobody slept that night.

After the sun was up and we'd made radio contact and were told that the choppers were at the launch site, Mac pulled out the waterproof camera.

"I'm going to build a blind and get some pictures of those guys," he whispered.

"Nothing else to do," I whispered.

"Very funny."

Mac made a blind with some pieces of wood and leaves and actually lay down about six feet from the trail. The interpreter sat behind him a few feet. I leaned against my pack and pulled out my note pad and pencil. Deak covered the rear and one direction of the trail, the interpreter covered the other direction.

Soon the sound of feet sloshing in muck appeared. The same two as the day before came down the trail again, talking to one another.

After they passed, the interpreter crawled back to me and said, "They talk about arc light, say very bad."

Sloshing again, louder this time. The interpreter crawled quickly back to his position.

They came walking side by side in the ruts. Two, three, four, ten, twelve, twenty-two, forty-four.

"Surely they must see my eyes, they've got to be as big as saucers." I squinted.

My heart was running a hundred yard dash again. I made marks on the note pad. "This is ridiculous." I kept marking beside M-16, AK-47, grenade launcher. "They've even got our grenade launchers." Khaki fatigues, boots. "Jesus Christ, is one of them going to see me?"

Mac was lying up there snapping away.

"How can they keep from hearing the shutter?"

Sixty-six, seventy-eight. They just kept coming and walking on by. "What will I do if one sees me? My field of fire is down the trail to the left. Oh shit, will a magazine be enough to give me time to reload?" Thump, thump, thump, thump. "Surely they must hear my heart beating, it sounds like a drum to me."

Ninety-eight, one hundred and twelve. About half were carrying white sacks like the VC we'd seen earlier. "I can't believe this."

There was a critical point at which each of them was most likely to pass his eyes over my location, if he were looking he would see me. I focused on the eyes of each one as he passed that point, watching for the slightest hint of recognition, the slightest wince, the most imperceptible twitch, the tiniest look of surprise. None came. "Have we turned invisible? Is this magic?"

One hundred twenty, one hundred thirty. "Two women. Must be nurses." Over two hundred and fifty NVA regulars passed by us. The last one moved down the trail and the last slosh of feet in water faded away.

Mac sat up smiling and pointing at the camera. He was ecstatic. "I got some great shots."

Fumbling with the camera, he rewound the film and popped the back open. "Shit!"

"What?"

He held up the camera. The film hadn't rewound. He held up the unwound roll. It was ruined.

Mac was sick. We were all sick.

We set a claymore in a crotch in a tree beside the trail, just within reach, and moved away to a huge log about twenty meters back and crouched behind it. Everybody needed a breather. Some breather.

"I didn't know there was going to be so fucking many of them," Mac whispered.

"They weren't saying much, just trudging along," I answered.

We spent our third night there. Nobody moved down the trail, except the same two who had been building the bunkers. They were still bitching about all the hard work.

"They must be permanent party," Mac said. "We could try to take them, kill one and try to capture the other."

"What about all the others?" I asked.

"Yeah, pretty risky," he whispered.

The next day was the same story, only this time we watched from behind the log.

Over a hundred had moved past, and it was close to mid day. One of the NVA yelled something and we all tensed up. The interpreter turned his head toward us and mouthed the words, "No sweat," and made feeding motions to his mouth.

The NVA moved a few feet off the trail, sat down and started passing bowls of rice around. Two of them leaned against the tree that the claymore was in.

My brain was racing. "This can't be happening, what if one of them has to take a crap and walks right into us?"

They sat and ate for fifteen minutes, which seemed like fifteen hours, then one of them said something and they all stood up and got ready to move out. The two who were leaning against the tree stood looking up at the crotch where the claymore was sitting. One of them pointed toward the claymore and spoke to the other.

Mac had the detonator in his hand. He looked at me and shook his head, "Yes?"

I shook my head no, furrowing my eyebrows.

He shook his head yes, I shook my head no. A couple of sweaty, mud caked mimes having a silent argument in the middle of the forest.

The NVA were still talking about the claymore.

Mac was quivering and shaking his head.

I mouthed "Wait," and watched to see if one of them would reach for it. The tension was unbearable. Sweat ran down my face and dripped from my nose. My armpits became waterfalls.

Finally they turned away and headed down the trail with the rest.

We all breathed deep silent sighs of relief, then waited to see if they would come at us from the side.

Nothing.

We got on the radio and told them the story. We'd been in four days. They told us to move back into Vietnam, they were going to pull us out.

Leaving the trail behind, we faded into the jungle, crossed the steam again without incident, and found a good landing zone back inside Vietnam.

After we were safely on board the slick and flying above the jungle toward Quan Loi, the crew chief told us they'd been on board their choppers and ready to crank up at a moments notice during our trail watch.

On the trip back to Quan Loi the chopper pilot flew the slick down a river just above the water. He rolled the chopper from side to side as he followed the twisting and turning river. When the river curved to the left, I was facing straight down into the rushing water, when he followed a curve to the right I was looking straight up at the sky.

We fired our rifles into the jungle and into the water every time the chopper turned on its side. I shot up most of my magazines.

We released a lot of tension.

Chapter 10

Stand Down

Back in Ban Me Thuot the officers in the Head Shed were pleased. We'd gotten in and out without being noticed, and had gotten some good intelligence on troop movements, weapons, and uniforms.

They told us about a mix up that had the place buzzing for a while. Somewhere in the relay of information, which went from us on the ground, to the FAC pilot, to the launch site in Quan Loi, where it was teletyped to Ban Me Thuot, or due to an error in my use of the SOI, they'd gotten the message that we'd seen an M-60 tank. They finally figured out that it was supposed to be an M-60 machine gun.

Four days and three nights without sleep and I hadn't felt a bit tired till the debriefing was over. Then my body wound down like an old watch. I was exhausted. I slept for eighteen hours.

Mail call brought a letter from home. My mother said that they were worried about me. The sheriff had told them that he'd heard I was missing in action, had been lost in a parachute jump.

I wrote home that this was ridiculous. I was alive and well, we weren't even making any parachute jumps in Vietnam.

Another letter from a friend told about the Beatles "Paul is dead" controversy. She mentioned the track on the *White Album* that you could play backwards and hear a voice that said "Paul is dead," and the picture on the new *Abbey Road* album, in which Paul is the only one barefooted, dead people don't wear shoes.

I managed to buy a reel-to-reel tape player and an amplifier and speakers at the PX. By this time there were some more records around and we borrowed them and made recordings. Iron Butterfly's "Inna Gadda Da Vida," Mike Bloomfield. Deak came up with the Beatles *White Album* and *Sergeant Pepper.* Somebody loaned us some Creedence Clearwater and Blood, Sweat, and Tears.

I was on stand-down so I was enjoying the time off. Rick and I had just smoked a joint and I had stepped outside to get some air, when the sergeant major caught me.

"Acre, go over to the TOC and show the general how to use the new web gear."

"Wha-a-a-t?"

"You heard me, get going."

You didn't argue with the sergeant major.

I stepped into the buzzing TOC and headed down the steps to the operations room. The colonel and a brigadier general, who was sitting on the edge of a desk, were talking casually. Power and authority radiated from each star on the lapels of the general's fatigues. His presence was obviously in command of the entire TOC. The colonel spoke before I saluted and formally reported.

"Ah, Specialist Acre, come show us how this thing works," the colonel said.

"Yes sir, I'd be glad to." I picked up the web gear and started snapping it on.

The harness was made of parachute webbing and had a couple of straps to hook under your legs, and a ring on top of each shoulder.

The choppers could lower ropes and pull you out of the jungle if you couldn't get to a landing zone. The old way of getting out on the ropes was to tie a Swiss seat out of rope and use a D-ring in front, as one did when rappelling. This new system was great because it was already on when you needed it, serving the double purpose of carrying your gear as well.

The general looked over the harness, asked if I liked it better than the old way with the Swiss seat. I said I thought it should be better and lots quicker, but hadn't had the opportunity to use it yet in the field.

"That was some mission you had the other day, pretty hairy," the colonel said.

"Yes sir."

"We got a lot of valuable information from that kind of close observation, keep up the good work."

"Thank you sir." We hadn't told them about the exposed roll of film.

When the general and the colonel were finished with me I approached a major who had been watching us talk about the web gear.

"Excuse me sir, I notice that our names are spelled the same," I said.

The major looked at my nametag, then said, "Yes, I guess they are."

"Well, I've just never met anyone who spelled their name the same who wasn't related to me, do you have any relatives in Eastern Colorado or Oklahoma?" I asked.

"No, I'm from Illinois," he replied blankly, and turned to some paperwork on his desk.

"Guess you must be the new head of Intel?"

"That's right."

"Well, just wanted to say hello," I said.

He nodded without looking up from the desk.

On the way back from the TOC, a guy I'd never seen before and never saw again stopped me and said, "Here, you might like this." He handed me a small reel-to-reel tape.

Before I could even thank him, he said, "Gotta go," and headed toward the TOC. He must have been part of the general's entourage.

"Well, how'd it go?" Rick was grinning.

"Oh, great, I just love to talk to generals right after getting loaded."

"It wasn't that big a deal was it?"

"No, no big deal, I didn't see you volunteering to take my place."

"Well, I had just smoked a joint, I wasn't going to volunteer, you're the one the sergeant major grabbed."

"OK, OK."

"What's that?" He pointed to the tape I was holding.

"Some guy just handed this tape to me and took off," I said.

"Hm, well put it on."

We liked the tape a lot. It was new music we'd never heard of. We listened to it for two months without knowing who it was. Nobody else recognized it.

One day we had Radio Saigon tuned in and the disc jockey said he was going to play some new music by a group called Crosby, Stills, and Nash. The melodious harmonics of "Suite Judy Blue Eyes" poured from the speakers.

"They are one person,

They are two alone,

They are three together,

They are for each other."

We recognized it immediately. It was the tape the stranger had given me. We always wondered who that guy was, and after we heard of the popularity of the album, how it came to be that we got it two months before Radio Saigon had it.

Chapter 11

More Stand Down

Somebody decided it was time for a party. It was constantly time for a party. Everybody who was off headed downtown to the bars and we drank like fools all afternoon and into the evening. The whiskey coke and Saigon tea had been flowing for a couple of hours when one of the girls typically accused the Grit of being a butterfly.

"Me butterfly, hail woman, I don't go tother bars, you're the butterfly!" the Grit resisted.

All the women at the table ripped into him in Vietnamese. He just grinned his big Texas grin and shook his head.

"Everybody is a butterfly," Rick quipped.

"Regardless, these women have everybody scoped out, if you go to another bar, they'll know about it before you get there," Watson argued.

All the men at the table agreed, while the women railed in protest again.

Then Nimzy spoke up, radiating his usual intensity, "I don't have to worry about bein a butterfly, cause I got the best woman in the whole damn city of Ban Me Thuot! No, the whole damn country, ain't that right Tui?" (Several years later, toward the end of the war, Nimzy would be one of the last defenders at the last stand of Kontum.)

Tui was sitting on his lap. He squeezed her closer, she smiled and nibbled at his ear.

She was extremely attractive, pretty face with long slender legs, shapely hips, pert grapefruit-sized breasts. I had designs on her myself, except for the trouble it would have caused with the women at the bar. Once they latched onto you, if you went for another one you'd wind up with none if you weren't careful.

"This gal, this gal will do anything for me, and I mean anything," Nimzy boasted.

"Ah, come off it," somebody said.

"No, no, I mean it, she'll do anything for me," Nimzy persisted.

"What will she do for you?" the Grit demanded.

"Well, I bet she'll even take a shit on my chest if I want her to!" Nimzy exclaimed.

We all roared with laughter.

"OK, laugh all you want to, here's fifty bucks says she'll do it," he contended, pulling fifty dollars from his wallet and slapping it to the table.

We looked at the money, then the Grit said, "OK I got ten dollars here, if everybody puts in ten we can match the fifty."

Each of us took out ten dollars and added it to the pile on the table.

"Looks like you got a bet."

"All right, that's gonna be the easiest fifty bucks I ever made. Come here Tui," he said, pulling her away from the table to talk privately.

"She's not gonna do it is she?"

"Looks to me like she's arguing about it."

"Hell, he'll just give her the fifty bucks."

"So what, we gotta watch if he's gonna collect the bet and she'll never go for that."

"Oh, yeah, yeah that's right."

Nimzy came back to the table. "OK ass holes, you've lost your bet."

"We gotta see it," said the Grit.

"You gotta see it?" Nimzy said, somewhat perplexed.

"Sure, how else you gonna prove it?"

"Ah, you pricks," he answered and returned to where Tui was standing.

"Boy she's arguing now," I said.

Nimzy returned to the table grinning, bent down and lowered his voice, "The only way we can all get past mamason is for you guys to pay for a short-time and take your girls upstairs."

"We can manage that," the Grit said.

"No problem," Watson agreed.

Everyone at the table stood up at once and reached for their wallets, producing the necessary eight hundred piasters for the trip upstairs.

On the second floor Nimzy and Tui went into one of the small rooms while the rest of us gathered around the door, which was left ajar. The women were all disgusted and withdrew to one of the other rooms and shut the door.

"Look at that body," the Grit whispered.

"I'll be damned, she's gonna do it!"

"She's doing it!"

Burkhardt stepped into the door of the bar, "B-50, let's go, we gotta get back to base!"

We piled into the deuce-and-a-half and the three quarter ton and headed for camp.

Just as always, about half way to camp we passed by the ARVN compound. Suddenly bullets were cracking over our heads, everyone was ducking and cussing.

"Those fucking ARVN's are sniping at us again!" White yelled. He was a big blonde headed guy who'd had his share of close calls in the field. He was working at the launch site in Quan Loi during his six month extension.

White was miffed. He jumped over to the minigun, aimed it high over the ARVN camp, and pulled the trigger.

Tracer rounds spewed like hot lava from the gun at four thousand rounds per minute. The old beat up truck sped down the highway ejecting spent brass cartridges like candy in a parade, with White standing at the minigun like a comic strip Red Baron, his scarf blowing in the wind.

The rest of us were hysterical with laughter, slapping hot brass out of our faces.

The truck stopped with a screech beside the club and we piled out to finish off the evening.

Inside the club I went to use the latrine. Moore was leaning against the bathroom wall, mumbling and staggering. I wasn't in much better shape, but I could still walk. I finished taking a leak and opened the door to leave. There stood the colonel. I shut the door in his face and grabbed Moore and stuffed him in a wall locker.

"Whatchew doin?" he protested.

"The colonel's coming!" I said, and pushed the door of the wall locker shut.

The only problem was, the colonel had simply come on in and was watching me try to convince Moore that he belonged in the wall locker. He was not amused.

The next morning all of Recon Company was up and in formation at 6 A.M. The sergeant major stood eyeing us from behind his bushy eyebrows, twisting his black handlebar methodically.

"Gentlemen, it has been brought to my attention that things got out of hand last night. A little matter of the commanding officer of the ARVN compound calling our CO (commanding officer), something about being attacked with a minigun." He raised his eyes, crossed his arms, and focused somewhere over our heads. "Anybody have anything to say?"

"They were sniping at us, Sergeant Major," a voice spoke.

"We just fired beside them," said another voice.

The sergeant major looked down at us again. "We just fired beside them," he mimicked.

He surveyed us intently. "The truck with the minigun will not be taken to town again! Is that understood?"

"Yes Sergeant Major," we said in unison, halfheartedly.

"Now, the following individuals will have the privilege of painting the new barracks for the next few days." He read a list of names that got us all. "Any questions? Dismissed!"

We broke formation and headed for our hooches, grumbling about the whole thing.

Next morning we were up early, getting our first day's painting in. One of the guys painted a grotesque sign on a piece of junk plywood and propped it up outside the barracks. The sign said, "The Army Teaches Over Two Hundred Skills." That was the Army's primary recruiting slogan at the time. The lieutenant wanted to know who painted it but nobody knew anything about it. It stayed there till we were finished painting.

Rick tuned in Radio Saigon on my transistor radio and we painted the day away. After a period of quiet he said, "It's just not fair."

"What's not fair?" I asked, "Hell, what are they going to do about it, send us to Vietnam?"

"Yeah, but we can't take the minigun to town any more," he smirked.

Then we were all singing (to the tune of "Oh Christmas Tree"), "We like it here, we like it here, yer fuckin A we like it here. We shine our boots, we shine our brass, we don't have time to wipe our ass. Even though we have malaria, we still police the area. We like it here, we like it here, yer fuckin A we like it here."

The lieutenant shook his head in dismay and walked back outside.

"What's the matter sir, don't you like the recon choir?"

We painters also had the privilege of pulling guard duty for several days.

A road followed the entire perimeter of the compound inside the berm. The Americans assigned to guard duty took turns driving around the compound all night. The SCU guards in the bunkers were supposed to wave when the jeep passed to show that they were awake.

By early morning we were thoroughly bored, so we made a race track out of it and timed each other to see who could drive the fastest around the perimeter.

While Rick and I were hot-rodding around the compound, a green pencil-thin snake slithered onto the road in front of the headlights. We stopped the jeep, jumped out and caught the thing and took it to the medic at the dispensary.

He immediately recognized it as a bamboo viper, a two step viper. There were two step and three step vipers. If the former bit you, you had two steps before dropping dead, if bitten by the latter, you had three steps before you dropped dead.

The medic cut off the head and dropped it into a jar of formaldehyde. It settled to the bottom, mouth wide open, thin, white, delicate, needle-like fangs fully extended, so sharp that one couldn't see the points.

Jerry was a Sergeant First Class and was the head of the dispensary. After pickling the snake, he and I visited for a while, and over the months we became friends.

He was balding, in his late forties, and on his fourth tour in Vietnam.

One evening I was at his hooch drinking scotch. He was in a depressed mood.

"What's the matter anyway?" I asked.

"Oh, I don't know, I just feel like I ought to be flying on the medevac choppers," he answered quietly.

A medic had been wounded that day. A SCU had been wounded on the ground, and when somebody was wounded they sent the medevac chopper in to exfiltrate the team. They were taking fire on the exfil and the medic caught a round in the upper arm.

I picked up a Smith and Wesson .38 that was lying on the night stand. "Why don't you use a .45?"

"I've had that a long time, bought it years ago, besides, a revolver is more fun," he said, smiling strangely.

"Very funny. How many tours did you say you're on?" I asked.

"This is my fourth, not counting extensions."

"Well, what the hell, after that many tours you have every right to stay out of the field, you've had your share of the shit."

"No, I still don't feel right about it."

He was not to be consoled.

Later he mentioned another problem. He had a wife and two kids in the States and was in love with a French-Vietnamese woman who worked in the PX at the 155 compound. I found out about this when he asked me to go downtown with him and buy a refrigerator for a friend of hers. He was out of punches on his card and wanted me to use mine to get the fridge for her. It was near the end of the month and I already had a fridge anyway.

He was just entering his second extension on this tour and he didn't think they'd let him extend again. He didn't want to leave her.

There wasn't much I could say. He showed me pictures of his wife and kids, whom he loved dearly. He loved the Vietnamese woman too, and was in the middle of a conflict he couldn't resolve.

A single guy could marry the girl if he thought that much of her and take her back to the States.

We unloaded the refrigerator in the woman's hooch near downtown Ban Me Thuot and drove back toward B-50 in silence.

I was watching the countryside and thinking that what everybody said was true. French-Vietnamese women were some of the most beautiful creatures in the world.

Jerry broke the silence. "Thanks, I owe you one, she really appreciated that."

"Don't worry about it," I said, "I've already got a fridge." I watched a lambretta loaded with bananas careen past the jeep. "Look at that guy leaning into those handlebars like he's on a cafe racer."

Engrossed in his own thoughts, he didn't notice.

"Jerry."

"Yeah?"

"How long have you been in the military?"

"Fifteen years, I was out for several years, then re-enlisted."

"What did you do when you were out?"

"I was in the construction business, built homes."

"But you came back to the Army, how come?"

He glanced at me, then looked back to the road. "I don't know, it's a long story."

"You didn't like the construction business, civilian life?"

"A guy gets used to the military life, and civilian life seems strange, besides it was hard to live with myself building homes."

"How come?"

"Oh, you build a cracker box that some poor bastard is going to spend half his life paying for, I just had a hard time dealing with the business. It just didn't seem fair somehow."

"What do you think about a young guy like me making a career out of the military?" I asked.

He shrugged. "I don't know, things have changed so much."

"How's that?"

He stopped the jeep for a farmer crossing the road with his water buffalo. "Oh, Special Forces isn't like it used to be. It was created as an enlisted man's unit, and the officers who were in were really dedicated people. Now all these officers run the show, most of them are just here so it will look good on their records." He put the jeep in gear and we started down the road again.

"What do you mean it was an enlisted man's unit?"

"Officers were mainly for administrative purposes, enlisted men made the decisions. Used to be you could have an officer removed for cause."

"For cause?"

"In other words you didn't have to have a reason, if he didn't get along, the enlisted could have him transferred."

"The EM really ran the show huh?"

"Yep, and it was a tight ship too."

We pulled to a stop at the gate of B-50, the guard waved for us to pass.

"Thanks again for the fridge."

"No sweat GI," I smiled. I got out of the jeep and walked to recon.

Jerry became a mentor of sorts. He'd explain the ins and outs of the military. He wasn't a lifer, to me he was a professional soldier. Men like him were the guidance and inspiration for us younger soldiers. Their influence emanated from character, not their rank. Because of this they didn't have to pull rank. Nobody wanted to cross a professional soldier.

I closed the door of our hooch behind me. Rick was threading a tape onto the recorder.

"What you got there?" I asked.

"Got this tape of Sergeant Shriver from one of the crew chiefs."

"No shit?"

Sergeant Shriver was a legend around B-50. He had disappeared with his recon team in the Fish Hook not long after the Tet of '69. The story said he carried two forty-five automatics, and someday he would come walking back into camp wearing nothing but a breechcloth and carrying a Montagnard crossbow. (Montagnards, or "Yards" as we called them, were the primitive tribespeople of Vietnam, so renowned as fine soldiers.)

Hanoi Hanna had broadcast special messages to him on Radio Hanoi, saying, "This time we will get you, Staff Sergeant Shriver, we know where you are going, we know you are going to Cambodia soon, and we will be ready for you."

On his last mission he took his SOI and maps, everything coded, out of his pockets and handed them to the chopper crew chief before disappearing into the jungle forever.

He had argued with the people back at the TOC about going in there, had said they'd never come back, it was just too hot. He was right, the whole team was lost. The bright light team that went in sustained heavy casualties, and hadn't found any sign of them. That was the last mission CCS ran into the Fish Hook.

"Well, turn the thing on, lets hear it," I said.

Rick got a couple of beers out of the ice box, popped the tops and handed me one. He pressed the play button on the recorder.

A voice drawled through the static, "This is Four Two, we're in contact, need some support." A chaos of weapons fire was in the background.

"Roger," the FAC answered. "Should have you some help in about one five."

The voice crackled again, "Sure glad to see you fellas, need some help azimuth six five, fifty meters."

"Roger, confirm azimuth six five, fifty meters."

"Roger." Pause. "That did some good, but we're still taking fire."

I took a swig of beer. "Listen to that guy, you'd think he was on a Sunday picnic!" I exclaimed. His voice was as calm and unwavering as if he was sitting in the room drinking beer with us.

"Sure doesn't sound like you, does he?" Rick said, with more than a hint of sarcasm in his voice.

We had played a tape a crew chief made of one of my exfils. I was shouting on the horn above the sound of the gunfire.

"No, I was pretty hyped up," I said.

The FAC came on again. "We're running out of juice and fire old buddy, going to have to leave you for about three zero."

Sergeant Shriver's voice came back immediately, "No sweat, we've got our CAR-15s and AKs here, see you when you get back."

The tape came on again, this time they brought in the Cobras along with the Huey gunbirds. They got the best of Charlie this time. The team was exfilled safely.

I felt pretty humbled after listening to the tape of his voice. It was difficult to imagine such calm in the face of death.

I started to watch for him, any day now, he'd come walking into camp, as dark as a Yard, barefooted, in a breechcloth, carrying a crossbow. It was easy to see.

Deak came back from the field with a souvenir. It was a piece of a packing crate that said "People's Republic of China," in English.

There was a lot of discussion about the role of the Chinese in the war. Several recons had reported seeing Chinese acting as advisors for the NVA. They were bigger men, with different uniforms, some with red berets.

Steve came back with reports of vehicles with red stars on their sides. The choppers had exfilled them from a really hot area, and the chopper people also had seen vehicles with red stars.

There was speculation about whether the Red Chinese would assume a larger role in the war.

Like everyone else, I wanted to capture a Chinese 9mm pistol. The Chinese 9mm was a beauty. It had a red star on the pistol grips. Unless it came from a cache, it would have to be taken from an officer.

The possibility of the Red Chinese coming down was a frightening thought.

Chapter 12

Steve: Bullshit, Truth, and Philosophy

Steve was an amazing person. He was an E-6 staff sergeant, and was running recon, as accomplished a one-zero as there was. It was his third tour. He knew the Army like the back of his hand. Sometimes it seemed he had the Army in the palm of his hand. He was intellectual, he was educated, he was valuable property for any commanding officer. He was an artist in the manipulation of military paperwork. If he wanted to be in Saigon on a particular day, he would get there. He knew the schedules of aircraft, he knew what papers to shuffle to get there. He was an expert. And he could handle officers, no matter what their rank.

I was in awe of the man. I was twenty years old. He was in his thirties. He knew the issues and could discuss the philosophy of pacifism or the inevitability of war, he could discuss politics, religion, history, finance, guerrilla warfare.

He asked if I wanted to ride into town with him one day. He'd arranged to trade some surplus equipment for some food. He was doing this as a favor for the mess sergeant, who was in need of supplies.

"How come we're having to go to the trouble of trading all this stuff," I asked him.

"It's just easier," he said. "They have more than they need of what we need and vice versa."

"Wouldn't it just be easier to requisition?" I asked.

"No," he shook his head.

"Why not?"

"Because this is a bastard unit. What's the matter, you tired of steak and shrimp in the mess hall?"

I liked to watch Steve when he was emphatic about something. His hands came off the steering wheel and he chopped the air with cupped hands.

While he listened to you speaking, if you were being serious, he'd look you in the eye for a minute to read you, then look to the side and nod his head while he listened, assuring you of his undivided attention.

"Bet you get tired of me always asking questions," I said, while looking out the side window of the truck. "I don't know much about what's really going on I guess."

"Oh, you're a pain in the ass," he chuckled, "but at least you're inquisitive, you think about things, a lot of people don't bother to think."

"Maybe I think too much," I murmured.

"What's bothering you?"

Squinting, I pretended to look out the window, then finally asked, "Are you afraid in the field?"

He looked at me questioningly.

"I mean, we all laugh and joke and have a good time and everything, go downtown and drink and play with the girls, but . . . ."

"Anybody who says he isn't afraid is either a liar or a fool," he said.

I nodded. I listened to the drone of the engine.

"I've been thinking about getting a tattoo," I said. "Put the C&C insignia on my arm, get a skull with a beret with crossed rifles underneath."

"You may have cause to regret it later," he said. "You might not want to be associated with this."

"Why?"

"You never know how they're going to react to this whole Cambodia thing."

"React? What do you mean? It's necessary isn't it?"

"Of course it is. They've got to have intel about what's going on over there. What I'm talking about is if the public sentiment changes and they condemn you for being here, you won't want the tattoo."

"Condemn me for being here?"

"It's possible," he said.

"Fuck, that's probably right."

We watched the Vietnamese scenery roll by.

"What did you do when you were a civilian?"

"I got a degree and went to work for an oil company in the Middle East."

"How come you came back in, I get so tired of all the military bull shit."

"You have the same bull shit in civilian life, working for corporate America, only there's more intrigue, things are less well defined. Nobody is wearing their rank on their lapel. If you can be a good soldier and understand the military system, you have as much freedom as anywhere else."

"That's hard to believe."

"You don't see it now, it takes time to gain a perspective. Have you read anything by Immanuel Kant?"

"No, just Descartes and Plato and Aristotle, I think Kant was the next semester."

"Well, Kant wrote a long essay called *Foundations of the Metaphysics of Morals*. At the end of it there is a short essay called 'What is Enlightenment?' If you read these and understand them, then you'll understand the professional soldier and the discipline and hardship he must endure, but also the personal mental freedom he gains as a result of his military discipline. It would help you see it. Then, for a completely different perspective, you should read a set of volumes called *The Life and Teachings of the Masters of the Far East*."

We were silent again for a few minutes. Finally, I said, "I guess I'm just trying to find answers, nothing is what it seems."

He nodded, "And truth is stranger than fiction."

"How do you see us fitting into this whole scheme of things, civilian life, politics, the military?" I asked.

"Fitting in?" he asked.

"Well, I mean, like right now there's a revolution going on in the States, they're protesting the war, and here I am in the middle of it. It's hard to know where we stand."

He looked at me intensely for a second. He shook his head as though frustrated. "First of all," he hesitated, "you're better off as a soldier not to have any politics. A soldier helps carry out policy, he doesn't make policy. I'm not saying to not have political opinions and an awareness of politics, you're just better off not letting politics, by politics I mean civilian politics, influence your judgment as a soldier. As far as what you call a revolution in the States, sure there are changes taking place, and there are a lot of people changing their minds about this war, but that's not our worry. We are part of the protective envelope that allows the political process to take place freely. You see, it's two completely different spheres of existence. There's no revolution taking place, just some changes. Here, you're on the very cutting edge of existence, your life is on the line, that's reality. The reality of what you're calling a revolution doesn't involve many people putting their lives on the line. They put pictures of Che on their walls and they fantasize. It's a fad that will pass. They're not really serious, pretty soon they'll get back to the realities of civilian life, which is making a living, and they'll realize they've got it better than anywhere else in the world."

"Then what would constitute a revolution, in your view?" I asked.

"A revolution would be if a Special Forces team took over the White House," he answered.

"Think we could take the Secret Service?" I asked.

"What do you think?" he said unequivocally. "Listen, don't expect anybody back in the States to appreciate what you've done. Modern society doesn't recognize its warriors, but they expect to be protected."

Chapter 13

Hey Jude

It was a sunny hot morning. I was packing my gear, getting ready to go in again. Rick came in quietly and sat on the cot.

"Hey, what's happening?" I said enthusiastically.

He looked at me with a serious expression.

"What's the matter?" I asked. I laid down the magazine I was loading.

"Got some bad news," he said.

"Bad news?"

"Mike is MIA."

I slumped on the packing crate and leaned against the wall and saw the moisture forming in Rick's eyes.

I remembered the last time I'd seen Mike, I could see him clearly, waving from the Blackbird as the door raised, on his way to CCN.

"So, what's the story?" I mumbled.

"It doesn't look too good. They got all the bodies out except his, everybody else was dead. Since they didn't find his body, he's listed MIA." His voice was strained and cracked.

It took awhile for the words to soak in. "So he's KIA then."

"Looks like it."

"I'm going to walk around a little," I said, after sitting with Rick for some minutes in silence. "See you after while."

"OK."

Grasping for the doorknob, I pulled myself up and out the door.

Suddenly it was foggy, the sunny day had turned dark and desolate. I stumbled out to the berm on the edge of camp and found a deserted spot, out of view. I sat on a stack of sandbags and stared blankly out at the jungle.

I could see him so clearly. He could have been standing there. Mike and his mischievous grin with his front tooth that was shorter than the other one. There he was, sitting at the restaurant table across from me, asking the waitress for that stupid vinegar and oil for his salad, nothing else would do.

I could see him at the snack shop in Fort Bragg, sauntering back from the jukebox, where he'd played "Hey Jude," his favorite song at the time. He never did say whether he had someone, but he played the song a lot. Looking out across the field of fire, beyond the tops of the trees, deep in the horizon, I could hear the music. "Hey Jude, don't make it bad, take a sad song and make it better. Remember to let her into your heart, then you can start, to make it better."

Something wet was running from my eyes and down my face. I started laughing. I stammered, chuckling, "You better not be dead, you son of a bitch. We've got a bunch of wrestling matches to have yet, and you haven't even shown me Huntington Beach, God damn it, you better not be dead!"

Company B at Ft. Bragg came back like a motion picture. A room for eight, his bunk beside mine. Almost a year spent in training. There was a river in front of my eyes. "Damn you, you sat beside me on the plane on the way over here!" I cursed myself for the thought I'd had on that plane, looking around me and wondering who would come back and who wouldn't.

Then I cried, as softly as I could.

I made my way back to the hooch, quietly singing "Hey Jude" to myself.

Rick was inside, cleaning his rifle.

"You want to go to town?" he asked.

"OK, I've got ten more magazines to stuff, then I'll be ready."

Chapter 14

A Gut Feeling and a
Snail's Pace

The SCU were roasting a duck over a fire. It was early in the morning. We were waiting to go in. We were on hold for a while. The C and C (Command and Control) chopper had been shot down further south. Our intelligence officer was on the chopper, along with a couple of other officers from the TOC. They'd been on an AR (aerial recon) of an operational area and a fifty-one caliber had shot the chopper down. Rick was on the team to retrieve what was left. The chopper had burned on impact. I didn't envy the job.

We were smoking and talking and watching the sun come up and hoping the clouds wouldn't box us in.

The duck's head was lying on the ground beside the fire, dead eyes staring blankly.

I lit a cigarette and picked the duck's head up and stuck the neck in my shirt pocket, so the duck appeared to be sticking his head out of my pocket. I stuck the lit cigarette in the duck's bill.

"Hey, don't forget to duck," I said.

"You morbid son of a bitch," Fast Eddie said.

The SCU were laughing and pointing at the dinky dau.

"Acre, how's your guts?" Fast Eddie asked.

"They're fair," I answered.

"I can't believe the medic let you go to the field," he said. "That amebic dysentery is serious shit," he laughed.

"Yeah, serious shit," I mimicked, "better hope you don't get it."

I'd spent two weeks walking back and forth to the latrine in thirty minute intervals. The urge hit like a thunderbolt in the stomach. "Guess since I'm down to every two or three hours, they figured it was close enough."

"Better hope those amoebas don't make it to your brain," he said.

"What do you mean? 'Hope they don't,' they already have."

We made it in without incident. This one was for three to five days. The main objective was a trail and possible base camp. The intel people wanted confirmation of enemy activity in the area.

We crept silently through another paradise. This one was full of underbrush, until we came to a stream. The underbrush along the stream had been cleared out. We came upon small grass hooches built beside the stream, so we pulled back and tried to skirt the area. There were signs of recent habitation and it was getting close to dark. We needed a safer place to bed down.

The team had to stop only twice for me to step off the trail and drop my drawers. Fast Eddie chuckled and pointed at me, stooped over with my pants down, trying to keep my weapon at the ready, straining under the weight of the radio-filled ruck.

I mouthed the words in silence, "Fuck you."

He just grinned.

At dusk we crawled into some brush and sat around a big tree. We set out the claymores and I got my pad and pencil out and got ready to report to the FAC.

Then we heard the distinctive sound of people talking in Vietnamese. Fast Eddie and I looked at each other. The SCU's eyes got big as basketballs. I turned the radio down as far as it would go and pressed the handset. My heart was pounding. The fear started in my gut and gradually worked it's way up my insides and into my head and out through my skin. I cupped my hands around the mike and whispered, "Belly Dancer, this is Hot Shot, over." I could hear the drone of the FAC plane in the distance.

"Hot Shot, go ahead."

I whispered the code number for enemy in close proximity. "Belly Dancer, we have a fiver-zero, that's fiver-zero, over."

"Roger Hot Shot, fiver-zero, it's getting close to dark, do you need a seven-fiver?"

I looked at Fast Eddie. We cupped our hands over one another's ear to whisper. "It's late, we're getting into a night exfil, think we can get out of here without them hearing us?"

A night exfil was risky. The choppers could be sitting ducks, it was hard to hit an LZ, getting and directing fire support was dangerous, if not impossible.

Fast Eddie thought for about three seconds and made the decision. He cupped his hands over my free ear, "We'd better wait it out."

I grimaced. I cupped my hands over the mike and hit the button, "Negative, Belly Dancer, negative seven-fiver."

"Roger, negative seven-fiver, out." The sound of the FAC plane faded into the distance and disappeared into nothingness. The silence and solitude fell into place like a sledge hammer. We were alone.

The sounds of conversation continued, rising and falling, with laughter occasionally. Then it would ebb and fade away, then rise again. Apparently they didn't know we were around, I hoped.

Maybe it was a con, just waiting for dark to come. What if they had our position already pinpointed? It was too late to think about moving now. They were too close, and it was too dark. They either had hooches just beyond the area we'd checked out, or they were moving through and had just bedded down. That didn't make sense, with the comfort of the hooches we'd seen so close, they wouldn't have stopped. We were near a campsite.

The darkness got so thick you could reach out and grab some. I waved my hand in front of my eyes. Nothing.

We sat there all night and hardly breathed. Charlie was over there smoking and joking. They were cooking something. We could smell the food. Couldn't see the fire though. I wondered how close they actually were. In the jungle ten meters can be a long ways, if the cover is right. It doesn't feel like a long ways. "Must have some ingenious way of covering their fires, wonder if they have ponchos," my thoughts even sounded too loud.

The night dragged on. I considered those guys over there, strange voices in the darkness creating nearly visual images. I wondered why I had no animosity toward them. In anger over Mike's death I'd vowed to kill a dozen of them, but in truth I would have liked to walk over there and say nonchalantly, "Hey, what's happening, you guys want to try some LRP rations?" They'd smile and wave me over to join them. I smiled at the craziness of the thought. I leaned my head back against the tree and listened to their chatter until they fell asleep. I couldn't help admiring Charlie's courage.

About midnight there was a familiar stab in my intestines. I grabbed my face and shook my head. No, it couldn't be true. But it was.

I reached over and poked Fast Eddie, then cupped my hands over his ear, "Guess what, I gotta shit."

I heard a faint gasp and a chuckle. He cupped his hands over my ear, "OK."

I pulled my arms out of the ruck and crawled quietly away from the tree. I didn't want to go too far, but didn't want to be too close either. After doing my duty and starting to crawl back, I realized that I'd lost all sense of direction. I could see only the thick darkness. I ran the short crawl back through my mind and tried to trace every move, the direction I'd turned when dropping my pants, every move. I crawled in the direction I hoped was correct. My hand groped ahead. I felt a foot, stopped, and dropped my head to the ground in relief.

When my arms were back safely in the ruck, I once again pondered the possibility of one small mistake that could cost one his life. Ten feet had unexpectedly become a mile.

The night slowed and stopped dead still. My contained fever pitch became merely stark terror.

Sometime just before sunrise I must have nodded off because Fast Eddie was poking me in the ribs. He pointed down the incline to where I'd crawled in the night. About five feet away from where I'd left my deposit, a huge snail was making its way toward the reward.

Eddie pointed at the snail and grimaced, making little nasal sounds of disgust.

I smiled.

Charlie got up and around and the voices started again. Fast Eddie was transfixed by the snail doing its slow motion dash toward the deposit. He'd turn away, then look again, then pull his lips into a frown, cover his face and look away.

"Would you stop snorting?" I whispered.

When the snail finally got there it climbed right up on top and started chowing down. This was too much for Fast Eddie. He wanted to get up and run so bad he couldn't stand it, but Charlie was still over there and we had to wait. Eddie put his face on his knees and shook his head. I smiled some more.

The voices quit a few minutes after we heard the FAC pilot overhead. I got on the horn. The FAC said they were pulling us out if we were OK. We didn't argue. We picked up the claymores, sneaked out, and moved a thousand meters or so away from the area.

We were exfilled without incident, except for Fast Eddie yelling at me over the sound of the chopper that it was the worst thing he'd ever seen in his life, "That shit eating snail, God damn!"

Chapter 15

Flesh and Spirit

The girls at the bar were glad to see us. We were glad to see them. I didn't miss Round Eyes much any more, the one's back home were busy with their college world. There was a letter occasionally, which got me dreaming a little, but the letters were hard to answer. The gulf between realities was broader than the Pacific.

In the bar there was no pretense, just some drinks and some fun. There was what could be called an occasional affair of sorts, but they were short lived, impossible romances in an impossible world.

The Cambode looked at Rick carefully, "You butterfly!" Her gold rimmed teeth sparkled.

Rick laughed, "No, I'm no butterfly, you're the butterfly, I've been in the field."

She slapped him on the arm, smiling, but sounding half serious, "You go other bar, butterfly."

Rick shook his head and laughed.

"You go Cambodia?" she asked.

"No," Rick answered, "just Vietnam."

She turned her head, keeping her eyes on his face. "I know, you go Cambodia."

"How do you know that?" Rick asked.

"I know, I know," she answered. The three women started jabbering to one another in Vietnamese.

Rick looked at me and shrugged his shoulders, saying, "Fast Eddie says you had quite a time."

"The night went by at a snail's pace."

He grimaced over the top of his whiskey glass.

"So, what did you find at the C&C chopper?"

"A burnt patch of ground, the chopper just melted away."

"Were they all in the chopper?"

"Yeah."

"Nobody jumped off before it hit?"

"Nope, it was sickening, just charcoal and bones. We managed to get what was left of them into body bags, but it was awful."

I looked around the bar. It was practically deserted. The bartender was leaning against the back counter, nodding off.

Ling and the Cambode were still talking. They were discussing something about Rick and me, but I couldn't make it out.

The Cambode spoke to us in English. "Rick, you (I was almost always referred to as 'you,' 'Ernie' was a tongue twister for them), come downtown tonight, stay hotel?"

We looked at each other.

"What about the MPs?" I asked.

"No sweat," Ling said, smiling, "No sweat."

"Think anybody will miss us tonight?"

"Nah."

We met the girls in the hotel lobby, which was a small room decorated with tiny, pastel colored, mosaic tiles placed in intricate patterns. They spoke to mamason, who stood guard sitting at a small table at the foot of a narrow winding stairs. She nodded and they motioned for us to follow them up. The stairs doubled back twice at each story. We followed them to the top floor.

I lingered at the stairwell, perusing the mosaic tile far below on the first floor, before joining the others in a large rectangular room, which held eight double beds arranged side by side. Each bed boasted a ruffled canopy that matched its bedspread. The beds were just far enough apart to squeeze in between.

On the other side of the room opposite the line of beds were various chests of drawers and standing closets. On top of most of the chests were small Buddhas or small shrines. The odor of burning incense filled the room.

Frilly, lacy things were everywhere, a collage of women's belongings, appearing soft and delicate against the mental backdrop of our own living quarters. We stood gaping at the room while Ling and the Cambode changed clothes, opening drawers and closets, putting things away.

"Can you believe this?" I said.

"I want to believe this," Rick answered.

I stepped out onto a balcony, which overlooked the buildings behind the hotel. It was at least forty feet to the ground. I could see no way out other than the narrow stairs. A heavy pipe rail circled the balcony. A vision came into my head, young women with their necks in nooses, hanging from those pipes, dangling lifelessly. I shook the picture out of my mind and went back into the room.

"There's no way out," I said.

"Nope," Rick said abstractedly. He was studying one of the little altars. It was a small Buddha about eight inches tall. A brass bowl sat in front of the Buddha. Beside the Buddha was a brass incense burner. All were placed on an ornate, hand stitched doily.

One of the girls set up a teakwood tray at the foot of her bed. On it were four wooden bowls, a large bowl of rice, chicken cut up in little squares, four glasses of water, several bananas and sweet mangoes.

They motioned for us to sit, then they took part of the food and put it in the bowl in front of the Buddha. After lighting some incense in the little burner beside the Buddha, Ling sat with us and we ate.

Other girls drifted in two at a time. Before long there were eight of them talking and laughing and giggling and arguing, changing clothes, opening drawers, looking into mirrors, wiping off makeup, things women must do everywhere.

I was surprised to feel so comfortable there amidst these women, things were so casual, we were accepted because the Cambode and Ling had invited us.

Evening came and we were still the only two men in the place. We wanted to smoke a joint. Ling led us into an adjoining room, which was empty except for a mattress in the middle of the hardwood floor.

I pulled the shutters back and peered out to the street below. It was almost dark and the traffic had stopped. The streets were deserted. The Cambode reached over my shoulder and pushed the shutters closed. She shook her head, telling me to stay away from the window.

We sat on the mattress and smoked the joint. The Cambode watched us pass the joint, shook her head no when it was offered. She made circles around her ear with one finger and said, "Dinky dau."

I laughed, "That's right."

Something triggered us and Rick and I became engaged in a serious conversation about philosophy or religion or something that seemed similarly profound.

We were talking intensely when the Cambode said, "Hey," slowly reached into her blouse and pulled out one breast, pulled out the other one, then pointed them both at us, holding one cupped in each hand. She was smiling teasingly and her gold rimmed teeth flashed as she looked first at Rick, then at me.

The discussion came to an abrupt halt. We both stared at the erect nipples erupting from the dark saucer-like areolae.

She dropped onto her back, still holding her breasts, laughing at the two statues in front of her.

Then we all were laughing.

"Guess we must have sounded pretty serious," Rick said.

"She probably recognizes pontificating ass holes even when she can't understand the language," I was wiping tears from my eyes.

The Cambode sat up, holding one breast this time. She said, "You look." She squeezed the breast and liquid came out of the nipple.

"I'll be damned, what do you make of that?" I said.

Rick just chuckled and said nothing.

A Vietnamese voice echoed in the stairwell. Ling ran into the room saying anxiously, "MPs come!" She motioned for us to follow. She led us back into the bedroom, and knelt beside the door. She pushed a panel in the wall to the side, which revealed a hidden closet near the floor. She quickly motioned that we should crawl inside. We did as she said, then as she closed the panel she put her fingers to her lips.

"Neat, huh?"

"This is unreal."

There was a thump on the panel and a "Shhhh!"

We heard men's voices speaking English and heard boots on the stairs outside the room. There was a sharp rap on the door, which one of the girls opened. The footsteps stopped beside us. We breathed slowly through our mouths.

"How's it going girls, everybody dressed?" said a leering voice.

It was answered with a barrage of insults in Vietnamese.

"OK, OK, you don't have any GI's hiding out here do you?" He stepped further into the room.

More outcries, with plenty of "do mams" thrown in. He walked around the room a minute, then walked past us again.

"Sorry to bother you, can't have any AWOLs you know." He went out the door. We heard boot steps going down the stairs.

We waited another few minutes, when a crack of light appeared at the edge of the panel. Ling slid it open and said, "OK, you come out now."

We crawled out of the space and stood up and stretched our legs. Women were all over the place in various stages of dress and undress, sitting around talking and smoking.

One of the girls turned the lights out. Ling lit a candle and set it on the table near her Buddha. I undressed, climbed into her bed, and lit a cigarette. It was nearly quiet outside, except for the sounds of distant mortar and artillery rounds. In a few minutes it was quiet in the room. The flickering candle made shadows on the walls and on the ceiling. The canopy over the bed seemed ethereal, floating.

Ling put some fruit and some bread into the bowl in front of the Buddha, then she knelt on a padded bench in front of it. She bowed her head and sat very still.

I contemplated her small form, illuminated by the yellow light of the candle. I wondered who she was. What thoughts were in her mind, in this strife torn land? I knew she must be helping support her parents and brothers and sisters and God knows who else, struggling to get some money together for her dreams, her future, whatever that might be. She became the embodiment of these suffering people, the focal point for this stranger from another land. The anguish of all her people radiated outward and I could see them all in a spark of intuition.

A feeling of gratitude, of being honored somehow, came over me. I felt thankful for a unique moment, and I saw, just at that instant, that home is in the heart.

She came to the bed and lay down beside me. We embraced and kissed, and let our passions meet.

I kissed her eyes and they were wet. I brushed the tears gently from her cheeks.

She snuggled close to me and we held each other in the stillness.

I lay watching the glowing candle, the flame gently swaying. The Buddha made fleeting shadows on the wall. Two spirits so close, so far apart. Two lives, two cultures, meshed, a moment's peace.

Chapter 16

Symbols

The commanding officer was a "good ole boy." He drank too much. The rumor was that he had lost a lot of men in some operation and had never gotten over it. He was a short, stocky man with a perpetually red face who never lorded it over the young enlisted men.

The XO was a different story. As the executive officer he was second in command, and was fond of pressing his rank on everyone. It was nearly beneath his dignity to lay eyes upon a specialist 4, much less talk to one. This miffed us, because those of us running the missions and getting shot at were mostly specialist 4s. The XO was a big imposing figure, well over six feet three, with an ego to match, who was forever pontificating about the methods of running recon, and expounding about the reason a given mission succeeded or failed. The fact that he'd never actually run a recon mission didn't seem to bother him, but it bothered us plenty. He was a textbook garrison officer, a lieutenant colonel, and it was obvious that this command was his key to full bird colonel and on up. He was a natural irritant to the field soldiers in the unit and was uniformly despised in recon company; the personification of the dichotomy that exists between the combat soldier and the administrative officer with a problem, to whom the act of war is, and remains, solely an abstraction, a body of theories to be manipulated mentally. A demonstrable example of this occurred while a recon team was in a firefight and one of the officers from the TOC was in the C&C chopper circling overhead. The officer instructed the helicopter pilot to "Take her down to a thousand feet, so I can be with the men." This little quote was repeated over drinks many times on many occasions by every SOG recon man at CCS. It became a cliché around Recon Company.

One day the XO went out to the firing range and fired an AK-47. On his second clip of ammo, the bolt in the weapon exploded out of the stock and flew behind him. He was lucky that he was firing it from the hip on automatic. If he had been firing it from the shoulder, the bolt flying back might have torn his head off. As it was, he was fortunate, the bolt missed his arm and his side.

Nothing much was said about it and no one was called on the carpet. It would have been nearly impossible to discover who had done it, especially since there were so many people to suspect. Privately everybody laughed about it. Maybe it would cool him down. He needed a brush with death.

Apparently someone had sneaked one of the explosive rounds packed with C-4 in with his ammo. It might even have been carelessness. He could have done it himself by accident, his shop was responsible for the psychological warfare hardware. Poetic justice.

The colonel, our commanding officer, had a cow and some pigs and some goats. The goats ran loose around the compound keeping the weeds trimmed off. Nobody would think of doing anything like the AK-47 episode to the colonel. He was OK.

Deak did paint a giant peace sign on the cow's side. It was three feet in diameter. The old cow was minding her own business, lazily chewing her cud, when the XO drove by in his jeep and saw her standing out there representing everything wrong with America.

He was already aggravated because so many of the young guys wore gold peace signs on gold chains around their necks. He was especially down on Deak, who wore the big pewter one directly under his chin on the short leather thong.

There was lots of ranting and raving about the cow's peace sign, but they never found out who'd done it. The old cow wore that peace sign for a long time. They tried to scrub it off, but it was good olive drab military paint.

I finally found a Rolex watch at the PX. It was a stainless GMT, not solid gold like the officers wore, but good enough.

Then several of us got the idea of having gold omega earrings made. The gold symbol was mounted on a gold stud so that the omega overlaid the earlobe. A medic friend pierced my ear with a hypodermic needle and inserted it through my earlobe.

After all, we were Project Omega and proud of it. We wore our gold stud earrings for several days before the talk finally reached the TOC.

The earring was too much. The XO roared. He said he wasn't commanding a bunch of mercenaries and we weren't going to look like a bunch of mercenaries.

One evening a couple of days later, while we were standing in line at the mess hall, we noticed a drawing had been put on the bulletin board that hung at the entrance. It was a sequence of illustrations portraying a peace sign gradually changing its shape, until it became a swastika.

"Hey Ernie, look at that would ya?" Deak laughed.

I didn't see any humor in it. "Pisses me off, can't wear my earring and look what they do to the peace sign."

"Eh, fuckem," Deak said.

It was hard for me to shrug off. That drawing symbolized the conflict in the U.S., and the polarization associated with it.

"Think they mean the Buddhist swastika-like symbol that the Vietnamese wear?"

"Whoever drew that probably thinks those Vietnamese are Nazis."

Chapter 17

Conflict

Duuring my fourth month in country we got a new commanding officer in Recon Company. This one was different. The other had been hardly visible, probably an efficient administrator, but otherwise unseen. This new CO, a captain, and a West Point graduate, seemed to know how to relate to us. The first thing he did was go through the records, talk to the SGM and other senior ncos in recon, and pick out the best one-zero we had.

That was Johnny Strange. He had been in more dangerous scrapes and gotten out of them in better shape than anybody else. He had something that gave him an edge. And Johnny was just a buck sergeant, an E-5. He was about six feet tall, blonde, serious, and quiet, and he seldom minced words with anyone.

The new CO of recon company ran five missions with Johnny, working as the radio operator, with Johnny in command of the missions.

Of course everyone in recon respected the man after he started running missions. He knew what we were doing. He was a leader. The respect was for the man and the rank; not just respect for the rank and contempt for the man. It made a difference. He could understand us, he could command us. He would listen to us, make a decision, give an order and it was followed.

He could laugh at our audacity in one breath, give an order in the next breath, and see the order followed. Maybe it would be questioned, or permission requested to discuss the order, but invariably followed.

When he decided that the whole company would run a mile before breakfast, except for people on stand-down, we grumbled and complained, but we did it, and we did it without hesitation, because he was out there in front of the pack, running with us, instead of telling an nco to lead while he went to breakfast. That was the difference. He was a rare officer.

One day he called everyone in recon together informally in the company meeting room. He was sitting in a chair at the front of the room. As we arrived he motioned for us to sit down.

There was a long silence. He swallowed hard and there were tears in his eyes. "I have some bad news for you," he swallowed again, "we lost Thomas today."

I felt numb. This was the first word we'd had about Thomas. We'd followed the exfil when they made enemy contact, but we'd not heard anything yet about casualties. Whenever a man was wounded he was taken directly to a hospital.

A voice wakened me from the dreamlike state of shock. The captain was talking to us. "It is particularly tragic because, as most of you know, Thomas just got back from R&R in Hawaii, where he'd been with his wife." He looked at his hands, which he held in front of him, fingertips touching, arms resting on his knees. He brought his hands to his side, then said, "That's all, you can all go back to whatever you were doing." He looked at the wall and waited for us to leave.

Thomas's roommate was especially shaken. Before this mission, Thomas had told him about his visit with his wife, and his decision that this would be his last mission, because he'd promised his wife that he would quit. The missions were strictly voluntary and one could quit if it got to be too much.

After the meeting with the CO, I went over to see Thomas's roommate for a while. He was sitting on a box, withdrawn, his eyes and face were puffy from weeping.

"Do you want to be alone?" I asked.

"I don't know," he answered quietly. He looked at the floor. He sat slumped, his already small body looking even smaller. Then he seemed to get a grip on himself and sat upright. He looked at me. "I know I don't want another roommate."

"How come?"

"Cause I'm a jinx," and he started to lose control again.

"What do you mean?" I asked, perplexed.

He looked at me searchingly with the most despairing look I'd ever seen and said, "Three roommates I've had, three roommates, and every one of them is dead." He named them, including Davis, ending with Thomas. "I tried to get him to move out, but he wouldn't believe me."

It was overwhelming, seeing the determination in his face, in the midst of such despair. I thought of that day soon after I arrived when he'd shown me the newspaper clipping in front of my hooch.

"You were rooming with Davis when he was killed?"

"Yeah."

"And you moved out of the room after he died."

"I just had to get out of there, like I said, I'm a jinx, thought it might change my luck."

"You're no jinx," I said. "It's just coincidence."

"I'll sleep in the rain before I have another roommate," he said.

He didn't have another roommate for the rest of his tour. Nobody, not even the SGM or the CO asked him to live with anyone. They let him have a room to himself.

I began to think more about my own mortality. Death was becoming as real as life. Sometimes sitting alone and pondering the situation I was in, I'd look at the uniform I was wearing, take the beret out of the wall locker and look at it. The rats had nibbled a couple of holes in it. I'd turn it over in my hands, feeling the suppleness of the green wool. I'd read the crest, "De Oppresso Liber," liberate the oppressed.

Then I'd look at the gold peace sign on my chest, holding it out away from my body between thumb and forefinger.

I thought of the sign in the club, "For those who fight for it, life has a flavor the protected will never know."

But, I believed in peace, I thought of my loved ones back home, about how much I really loved them, more than any of them would ever know.

I felt caught, somewhere in some irreconcilable middle.

I reached over to the stereo and ran the tape forward, looking for a Beatles' song that was especially poignant.

"Boy, you're gonna carry that weight, carry that weight, a long time."

Chapter 18

Solutions

There was an occasion sometime after Rick went on the mission to recover the bodies from the downed Command and Control chopper, when I went to the laundry to pick up my clean fatigues.

The Vietnamese man who ran the laundry laid my fatigues on the counter, nodding his head and smiling. I examined them to make sure they were all there and were the right ones. On the bottom of the pile he had added three pairs that had embroidered instead of stenciled name tags and CIB's, with major's insignia sewn on the lapels. They belonged to the major at the TOC who had gone down in the C&C chopper.

Saying nothing, I pointed to the major's oak leaves; the distinction was obvious between my fatigues and the others.

He pointed to the identical names on both sets of fatigues, started talking urgently in Vietnamese, waving his hands rapidly toward the door, saying, "You take, you take!"

I shrugged my shoulders, picked up the pile of fatigues, and headed for Recon Company. Vietnamese could be very superstitious.

I cut the major's patches off the fatigue blouse and put specialist 4 pins in their place. The fatigues were a perfect fit. I asked Rick what he thought of my new uniforms.

"They look great, where did you get them?" he asked.

"They belonged to the major, they were still at the laundry," I answered.

"You're crazy."

"Oh, come on, you're not superstitious are you?"

"Is that your way of defying death, wearing a dead man's clothes?"

"Nah, I just thought embroidered name tags were neat. Anyway, the guy at the laundry insisted that I take them."

"Bull shit. You're still crazy!"

Unlike some other people, I didn't save much money. Some guys sent nearly everything they made home, with the idea of buying a new car, or just having a savings account. Having some set goal back in the World made it easier to cope. I spent my money, not only for the stereo and the watch and the refrigerator for our hooch, I spent it downtown. I ate at the restaurants, I drank at the bars, I went to the massage parlors, I bought things at the PX. I lived for the day.

Yet I immersed myself in the music from the World that we managed to accumulate.

The Beatles reached the height of their creative powers. Crosby, Stills, and Nash were speaking for a generation of young Americans. Bob Dylan was cutting the establishment apart with his searing verse.

As the months passed, I clung to my vision of what was going on in the States. I thought there was a revolution going on, the values of the nation were changing. We would be leaders in the world to start an age of enlightenment and peace. I was twenty-one years of age.

Everyone had his particular ways of coping. Some of us escaped into the music and getting high, some drank, some wrote home faithfully to a wife or loved one, keeping his link with the World as tangible as he could. Some had or developed deep religious faith in God, in Christianity. I developed a religious awe of existence, which launched my thoughts into a painful investigation of matters religious, but I rejected any form of conventional religion. I came to envy the SCU who wore a little Buddha on a chain around their necks, and when in enemy contact they would put this little Buddha between their teeth. They believed that it kept them from harm. One of the Yards swore that with the Buddha between his teeth he could see the bullets coming at him in time to get out of the way. I asked him if he meant tracers, and he emphatically said no, he could see the bullets.

Then there were those few who lived for the experience, the adrenaline rush, of being in the field and being in combat. And I could understand them, for there was nothing to compare with it. Eyes were never clearer, hearing was never more acute, smell was never more discerning, the body was never more alive.

Perhaps these men were really the best field soldiers, for they relished the act of going into the field. But I saw what happened to some of them, and hoped I could keep myself from being like them.

Frank, for example, was a good soldier, who had been in Laos and all over Southeast Asia, involved in clandestine operations from the start. But he could barely survive garrison life, had been in the military for years, and was perpetually a specialist 4. Drink was his solace, and though he could expound as good a conservative philosophy as any republican politician, and could play chess like a master even when he was dead drunk, he was reduced to the barbarity of wearing, on a string around his neck, the ear of an enemy he had killed.

On one occasion at the bar, one of the girls annoyed him, so he reached over and picked up her Saigon tea. Holding the drink close to his chest, he stirred it with the dried up, wrinkled ear, laughing scornfully at her indignation.

Another individual was a man we called Babysan. He was a staff sergeant, and like Frank, drank huge quantities of alcohol. Babysan came to our unit after I had been there about six months. Babysan was famous. He was on his fourth tour, and had run recon every tour. He was considered the best of the best. He had well over sixty missions to his credit. He wouldn't say exactly how many, but I suspected the facts would show closer to a hundred and sixty. He was a short, small framed man, with the advantage of being not much bigger than most of the Vietnamese. After a couple of days in the field the reddish stubble on his face looked incongruous growing on his baby-face. He knew tactics and escape and evasion, and could inevitably predict and intuit what the enemy was going to do. No one would hesitate to go to the field with him.

However, when he was drinking he became morose, and bemoaned the fact that he could never go back to the States, could never adjust to garrison military life, or civilian life.

When in base camp he was like the rebel without a cause, and his knowledge of the military, and his disdain for many of the officers, made him disliked by the majority of them. Yet he continually proved himself in the field.

Something about Babysan made me suspect that indeed, he would never return to the States, he was so adept at his craft, and so totally absorbed in it. He had nothing else.

Then there were the professional soldiers like Steve, and a couple of other senior ranking non-commissioned officers who were running recon, who provided leadership for the majority of us lower ranking soldiers, who were courageous in the field, and had the tenacity to cope with the problems of garrison life, even if they didn't prefer it.

These men had obviously faced the same questions I was facing, and had overcome the driving force that managed to push some over the edge. There was a quality about them, the way they carried themselves, the look in their faces, a solidness about their countenances, a clarity in their expression, which made them rocks amid the chaos.

The highly charged atmosphere in which we lived accentuated men's weaknesses, stretched the limits of behavior, developed or destroyed character.

I wondered which way I would go.

Above and beyond and despite the broad differences in our politics and our ages, our attitudes and our personalities, the one thing that was most basic to our survival was the deep camaraderie that linked us as Recon Company.

Chapter 19

Disillusion

Charlie was more than an abstraction. I walked in his deserted camp-sites, saw the grass hooches and stores of rice, saw clothes hanging to dry on sticks in the ground, examined trenches and bunkers that he'd built. I huddled close to him and listened to him talk in the night, I sat on trails and watched him walk by.

I began to question his motivation when I saw the hardships he endured. Why did he fight on in the face of superior fire-power? Why did he walk down the miles of trails and live in such primitive conditions in the middle of the jungle? I knew how hard it was to exist in the jungle, the heat and the insects and the snakes and the rain, and I was only inserted for a few days, then pulled out by the choppers. I didn't have to live there like Charlie did, or like some of the guys in our own conventional forces.

One day I was inspecting the barracks of my SCU team, as we were required to do periodically, and was engaged in a conversation with my interpreter. Tai was a diminutive man even for a Vietnamese, older than most of the men in recon. He was well past thirty, and usually reticent.

During this exchange I tried to lead the discussion toward politics, as I had before and gotten nowhere. "What do you think about the Americans being here?" I asked.

Usually he responded with a nod and a "number one." This time he just shrugged and looked away, saying nothing. I waited. By this time we were pretty well acquainted. Perhaps he trusted me a bit.

Finally he said, "The Americans will leave, just as French did."

"Just as the French did?" I asked. "You mean Dien Bien Phu?" I wanted him to elaborate but he would not. "What about democracy in South Vietnam?" I asked.

He smiled ironically. "Who is father of your country?"

"The father of my country?" I hesitated, wondering why he asked the question, "Why, George Washington I suppose."

"Yes, George Washington," he nodded, "Ho Chi Minh is father of my country."

I was astonished. This was my interpreter, with whom I had been to the field many times. After a silence, I asked, "Do you really mean that?"

He smiled his best oriental smile, the lines in his face turned upward, "No worry."

"Why are you fighting on this side?" I asked.

He studied me a second. "This my home, I work where I can work, feed my family, I do good job for you. You ask me politic, I tell you, we friend. No worry, we go field, we friend, I do good job."

Chapter 20

Fatalism Fifty-one Caliber

The little toe I broke that first morning in Vietnam continued to ache. It served as a reminder, a focal point, of that first day in country, which seemed far in some hazy and distant past.

The CAR-15 had become an extension of my arm, as vital to my life as my hands and heart.

On moments of reflection midway through the chopper flight to the point of insertion, I would mentally calculate the time necessary for the choppers to get to us, the time I would have if I got hit, ten minutes, twenty, thirty, before the choppers could get into the area. I rationalized the possibility of catching a bullet, "They'll have to get me in the head or the heart, otherwise I'll have a good chance."

On one insert into Cambodia, the landing zone was very small. So small the chopper had to hover straight down amidst the trees. This was difficult for even the best of pilots.

The chopper descended down into the tiny open area. The pilot hovered as close as he could to the elephant grass and realized that he could get no closer to the ground. The rear rotor was dangerously close to the trees, and the front rotor was swishing ever closer to a bone-white weathered tree, which reached out menacingly.

The crew chief yelled to us above the noise, "You'll have to unload, we can't drop and we can't go back up, too much weight."

I looked down at the billowing elephant grass. There was nothing else to do. I jumped from the skid and fell toward the ground. It was farther than it appeared, twelve feet at least. I hit the ground hard and did a parachute landing fall as best I could, landing on my back.

There I lay, looking directly above me at the chopper slowly rising vertically amidst the trees. My comrades were picking themselves up and running into the trees away from the landing zone. The fall had knocked the wind out of me and I couldn't seem to move. I lay there for a moment, realizing just how heavy the ruck was. The absurdity struck me like a hammer and I heard the sound of my laughter above the thrashing of the chopper blades. For a moment, time stood still, warped, or something, and I lay there amused at my helplessness. "I'm a turtle on its back!"

In a few seconds I got my wind, got to my feet and ran toward the others, listening and watching like a rabbit in an open field, still laughing at the overturned tortoise I'd been a moment before.

During the briefing before the insertion, we were shown an area that was thought to be an enemy base camp that included fifty-one caliber positions, lethal to helicopters.

The purpose of the mission was to approach the camp, find a main trail nearby, and watch enemy movements. If there were no movements, then we were to venture close to the camp, determine if it was occupied, and if it was deserted, examine it to establish if it was being used, or how long it had been deserted, and what the camp was used for. Whether it contained mock-ups of helicopters and tanks, training areas, target ranges, obstacle courses, how many troops it could accommodate etc.

We moved toward the target area with a minimum of resistance from underbrush, and soon discovered that the area was honey-combed with well-used trails. As we neared the objective, the tension mounted, something was definitely going on over there.

About a thousand meters from where the camp was supposed to be, the jungle disappeared. To our left was a huge field, a half mile across, which was cleared and cultivated. Adjacent to the field was a little building that reminded me of the roadside vegetable stands one sees in the U.S., except its roof was grass and its walls were made of bamboo. We were fascinated by this hooch, because the side hinged down to form a serving window, like someone was open for business right in the middle of nowhere. Peering inside through the window, we saw that it was piled full of gourds, huge cantaloupe-sized cucumbers, and other vegetables that had obviously been grown in the huge plot. Away from the hooch and disappearing downhill into the jungle meandered a trail wide enough to accommodate a truck.

We had to decide what to do. We could go on downhill in the general direction of the trail, or we could backtrack and try another approach. We certainly couldn't cross the field. The dilemma was solved for us.

Up the trail came an NVA soldier, alone. He saw us, turned around and ran, screaming. In a few seconds we were taking fire from his direction. We had little choice. We headed into the jungle right beside the field, between the field and purported base camp. I got on the radio. In a matter of minutes Charlie would start sweeping the area, pinning us against the field.

The choppers were over us in ten minutes, ready for fire direction. I asked for and got a barrage of rockets and minigun fire in the direction from which we were taking fire. I said emphatically, "Fifty-one cal! Break away over the open field! Base camp! Break over the field!"

After making a gun run, the gunship would go into a steep bank to turn around, when it would be most vulnerable to ground fire. It was important for the people on the ground to warn the choppers of the location of enemy fire.

It was a great relief to see the hail of bullets and rockets when the gunbird flew across, laying down the barrage in exactly the spot I'd asked for. The fire from the area quit immediately.

Then my heart sank. The gunbird finished its run and banked, not to its left over the field, but to the right, over the base camp. Streaks of white sprayed through the air like a supercharged Roman candle. Fifty-one caliber.

The FAC came on the radio, "We've got to leave you a minute, we've got a chopper down, will you be OK?"

"Are they close enough for us to help?"

"Negative," came the reply. "They're two clicks away from you, on the other side of the camp."

"See you later," I answered bleakly.

It fell silent around us. Apparently the miniguns had gotten whoever was after us, or they'd gone after the downed chopper. A downed chopper was a big prize.

In the distance we could hear the roar of miniguns and the explosions of rockets. We could also hear the steady thump of the enemy fifty-one caliber.

I whispered to Fast Eddie, "Why didn't they break to the left, you heard me tell them didn't you?" I was nearly frantic, needing confirmation that I'd warned them.

Fast Eddie nodded his head, "Maybe they were wanting to draw fire." He put his finger to his lips.

I listened intently to the radio. The crew chief of the gunbird had caught a fifty-one caliber in the head. The chopper was down in rough terrain. The medevac chopper, with the Special Forces medic, hovered over the area of the downed chopper, dropped a rope ladder, and the medic climbed down the ladder and went to the aid of the crew. No one else was severely injured, but they were in shock from the crash. The medevac chopper started taking fire from the woods. The medic got the crew organized and had them lay down a field of fire with their M-16s while he picked up the crew chief and carried him up the rope ladder into the hovering chopper!

I couldn't believe my ears. Climbing a rope ladder into a hovering chopper is no easy task, this guy carried the crew chief up that ladder. Everyone else got out safely.

In about a half hour the FAC was back talking to me, asked how we were doing. I said OK.

The gunbirds made runs like thunder crashing all around while a Huey landed in the field behind us.

This time the gunships broke away to the left, over the field.

The Huey left the ground, gained altitude, and we were away.

Intel now had confirmation that the camp was populated, and that there were fifty-one calibers, but it had been costly.

Back on the ground at Ban Me Thuot, the pilot of the slick motioned me back toward his helicopter. An Army helicopter unit that I wasn't familiar with had pulled us out and I'd never seen this pilot before.

"That was a pretty hairy mission in there," he said.

"Yeah," I answered.

"I'll write you up for a silver star, and you write me up for one." His statement was partly a question.

I looked him in the eye while my mind considered the brave medic and the dead crew chief. I picked up my ruck, slung it across one shoulder, turned and walked toward the jeep waiting to take us to debriefing.

Chapter 21

A Party and a Promise

W e managed to get things pretty comfortable in our room. Rick had his feet propped up beside the old desk we'd found, listening to Mike Bloomfield on the stereo. He was busy writing a letter. I was reading an article about Special Forces in a man's adventure magazine that was circulating around recon company. The article was about a Special Forces recon team that was trapped in a cave, getting shot at by Viet Cong.

"Rick, listen to this," I yelled above the music.

He reached over to the stereo and turned down the volume. "Whatcha readin?"

"This is, I'll have you know, an actual account of a Special Forces Recon team. Listen to this, 'The young sergeant fired his M-16 at the advancing enemy, rat, tat, tat, but it was useless, the enemy's AK-47s thundered and overpowered them.' How do you like that? The young sergeant and his rat, tat, tat."

Rick laughed, pointed his finger at me and said, "Rat, tat, tat."

"You think that's bad, how about this? 'They were nearly overcome when the lieutenant rushed the advancing enemy with his BAR, the powerful boom, boom, boom, mowing down everything in its path.'"

"Let me see that," Rick said, and grabbed the magazine. "Since when do lieutenants get boom, boom, booms while young sergeants get only rat, tat, tats?" He laid the magazine on the desk and read the article, shaking his head in disbelief.

"Look at the cover," I said, "True story."

Deak came bounding into the room, full of his perpetual enthusiasm. "I've talked to everybody and they're all up for it."

"All right!" we both exclaimed.

The party was on. I ran over to my wall locker and dug out a set of SCU fatigues. Rick did the same, then held up the pants, and threw them back into the locker.

"Mine are too long, give me a pair of yours," he said.

"Let her roll up the cuffs," I said, then tossed him a pair of mine.

The three of us jumped into the three quarter and headed for downtown.

At the bar we got all the girls together that everyone had asked for. We explained the whole thing to mamason. She shook her head no, no, no, while chewing her betel nut rapidly, making her teeth seem even more purple. She finally relented, after we agreed to pay her double in advance.

Then we herded the ten girls upstairs and handed out the fatigues. They were all laughing and having a great time of it, a new adventure. After they were all dressed, we passed out the bush hats and helped them tuck their hair up into them. We inspected them all the make sure they looked OK.

"Rick, the Cambode's tits are too big, she'll have to slump in her seat."

"Too big! Do Mam!" She slugged me on the shoulder.

We got all the girls loaded into the back of the truck and headed back to camp. If we could just get by the guard post.

We pulled up to the sentry, who stopped us, looked in the back of the truck, saw ten SCU, and waved us on. He was grinning from ear to ear.

We drove by the TOC quickly. A major was sauntering up the walk, but he didn't give us a glance.

We made it.

We pulled the truck into recon company. The girls got out and we put them in our room. We broke out the booze and the party was on.

We joked and laughed and drank for a couple of hours, then the crowd started thinning out, people pairing off and going to the various hooches.

Rick, the Cambode, Ling, one extra girl, and I were left in our room. Deak took his girl to the Grit's room. The Grit was in the field. We were out of cokes, so I headed to the club to buy some.

At the club, I noticed Jim was sitting at a table by himself looking glum. I sat down across from him.

"How's it going over at the bright light?" I asked.

"Oh, OK," he said. "I don't like it, I still wish I'd been assigned to recon, they still won't let me transfer."

I laughed. "Yeah, I remember all the flack you gave them."

"Listen," he leaned toward me, "I want you to tell my dad to name a bull after me."

"What?"

"If I don't make it out of here, by God, you tell my dad to buy the best bull he can find, and to name that fucker 'Jim.' Will you do that?"

"Come on Jim, don't think like that," I protested.

"God damn it! I'm only half drunk and I'm serious," he raised his voice and looked me straight in the eye. "Will you go see my folks, and tell my dad to name a bull after me?"

"Yeah, I'll go see them Jim," I nodded.

"Well, you go see Mary Ann too, she feels like she knows you."

I nodded again, looking at a spot on the table. His girl friend always said hello to me in her letters, and I'd throw in some remark to her when Jim was writing her back at Ft. Bragg. She'd even sent me some home made cookies one time. I smiled, remembering the time she sent Jim a birthday cake. When he cut into it, there was a pint of his favorite bourbon inside.

"Jim, you're going to make it all right," I said.

"Damn it, just promise me you'll go see them!" He was even more emphatic.

I looked at his face. Behind the alcoholic haze was a despair like I'd seen in Thomas's room mate's face.

"OK Jim, I promise."

"Thanks, it means a lot to me." He took a big swig from his glass.

"Come on over to recon, we sneaked a bunch of girls on post and there's an extra. Come on over will you?"

"You sneaked girls on post?" he queried. He looked a little happier.

"Yeah, and we got one too many, come on over."

"I might be over later," he said.

"No maybes about it, come on over and party with us," I picked up the six pack of pop from the table and started for the door. I turned toward him, "They'll probably want another speech in Provo, you know."

He smiled then, but kept his eyes on the table in front of him.

On my way back across camp I thought about Jim. My steps were lit by the yellow light of the illumination rounds that perpetually drifted on their little parachutes around the perimeter of the camp.

During leave, before coming to Nam, Jim had flown to Provo, to see his girl friend, who was in college. When he stepped off the plane, a couple of representatives from the college approached him and said, "Your car is waiting sir."

Jim shrugged his shoulders, said fine, and followed them to the waiting car. They drove him to the university. En route he discovered that they had been waiting for a colonel who was to give a talk to an auditorium full of college girls. Apparently they didn't know the difference between a specialist 4 and a colonel. Jim just went along with it, went with them to the university, let them introduce him as the colonel, got up on the stage and gave an extemporaneous talk to the girls. His girl friend, who was in the audience, was mortified. Jim was the only one who was amused when the real speaker finally made it to the auditorium. He'd used one of his favorite expressions, "What were they going to do about it, send me to Vietnam?"

I opened the door to our room. Buffalo Springfield was singing, "There's a man with a gun over there, telling me I've got to beware, I say, stop, hey, what's that sound, everybody look what's going down."

Rick was stirring a casserole of LRP chicken and rice and C rations. I put the pop in the fridge and mixed myself a drink.

"Jim's coming over, he's bummed out tonight."

"What's he bummed about?" Rick asked. He dipped the spoon in the concoction and smacked his lips.

"Oh, I don't know, just in a bad mood, depressed."

"Tui will cheer him up." Nimzy was in the field but Tui had wanted to come to the party anyway, leaving her unattached for the night.

"I hope so, she could sure cheer me up."

We had just finished chowing down on the chicken and rice concoction when the door flew open, a stocky figure leaned against the door frame, then stumbled into the room, managing to fall back against the door, slamming it shut behind him.

"Hey Frank, how's it goin, you win at pinochle tonight?" Rick asked, turning his head and smiling broadly. He had his hands behind his head, elbows back, leaning against the wall.

"Hmmm," Frank moaned, eyes shut, head resting against the door.

"Well, come on and sit down and party with us," I said, devious thoughts taking shape.

Frank made no effort to move, so I took his arm and pulled him to a chair across from me, then set up the make-shift table between us. He immediately plopped his head on his arms on the table.

"What are you doing?" Rick asked, wrinkling his brow.

Enemy heavy machine gun, at 5th Special Forces museum in Nha Trang

David Davidson (Babysan), the best of the best, KIA

Headquarters, 5th Special Forces, Nha Trang

Author at CCS base camp

Author just back from a mission

Downtown Ban Me Thuot

Bill Coughlan with interpreter
(right)

Recon Company, Command
and Control South
(lower right)

Ron "Deak" DeCarlo (below)

M. Sgt. Tony DeLuca,
killed while trying to buy
POWs out of Laos

One of the Omega earrings
mentioned. (left)

"Fast Eddie" Helfand
(left corner)

Hinkel and Graham in dis-
guise, headed for Saigon and
time off
(below)

Johnny Strange
in a reflective moment

Air Force "Green Hornet"
gunbird. Note the minigun
in the door

Rick Hinkel

Riding the ropes on the
Maguire Rig

Last day in Nha Trang
before heading back to the
world; the runways took
incoming (left)

Getting ready for one
of our practice jumps
before the night
infiltration.
Chinese Nung, author,
and Babysan (below)

Downtown Ban Me Thuot (above)

Rappelling out of a chopper. Note how
high the chopper is (right)

Our red
"living room."
DeCarlo, Hinkel,
Helfand relaxing

The team that invited
the author to the
party for Buddha

My point man

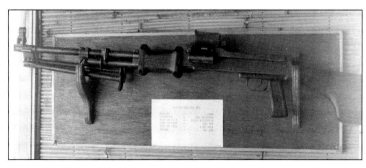

Enemy machine gun, at 5th Special Forces museum in Nha Trang

Sgt. Maj. Matamoris

Sign reads, "The essence of courage is not that your heart should not quake but that nobody else should know that it does. – E.T. Benson" at Museum Nha Trang

The "Nungs"

The Blackbird (right)

Sign at the Museum Nha Trang (right)

DeCarlo, Hinkel, Bouldin, Hensley,
Graham going to town (below)

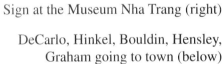

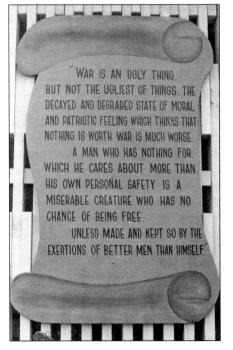

"WAR IS AN UGLY THING.
BUT NOT THE UGLIEST OF THINGS. THE
DECAYED AND DEGRADED STATE OF MORAL
AND PATRIOTIC FEELING WHICH THINKS THAT
NOTHING IS WORTH WAR IS MUCH WORSE.
    A MAN WHO HAS NOTHING FOR
WHICH HE CARES ABOUT MORE THAN
HIS OWN PERSONAL SAFETY IS A
MISERABLE CREATURE WHO HAS NO
CHANCE OF BEING FREE.
    UNLESS MADE AND KEPT SO BY THE
EXERTIONS OF BETTER MEN THAN HIMSELF"

"I'm getting out the chess board," I said, grinning with evil intent.

"That's not fair! Hell, he's drunk on his ass," Rick exclaimed, laughing.

"I figure the odds should be just about even, Frank's dead drunk and I'm buzzin. I mean I'm electric! Frank, you want to play a game of chess?" I asked in mock sincerity.

"You kabeeme," came a muffled reply from the drunken face buried in its arms.

"What's that Frank?"

The broad flushed face raised from the table, bleary eyes focused slowly at my beaming anticipation, the lips formed the words with difficulty, "You can't beat me," and the head fell back to the table. "You want white, Frank?" I asked, while setting up the board.

"You take white."

"OK, I moved, it's your turn."

Frank raised his head enough to see over his arms, laboriously reached for a pawn and moved it one space forward.

This continued for several moves. Me in my electrified state, trying to encompass the entire board in some intuitive strategy, then prodding Frank to wake up and move his piece.

"Hey, it's your move again Frank." No response. I reached for his arm and shook it gently. "Frank, it's your turn."

Once again he raised his head, peering about as though he'd forgotten where he was.

"Come on Frank, it's your move," I said impatiently.

He concentrated momentarily on the chess board between us, moved a bishop across the board, dropped his head back to the table, and said "Checkmate."

"What?" I said in astonishment.

"Checkmate," said the barely coherent voice.

"Yeah but," I pored over my king, which I had left open to the diagonal with no way to move or to block the attacking bishop. "God damn it!" I exclaimed.

Rick got a kick out of my frustration, "How many moves was it, eight?" He laughed and laughed.

"Seven," said the voice from beneath the folded arms.

"What did I do wrong Frank?" I asked.

"Give me a break," Rick said, "look at your king, you left it wide open."

"Yeah yeah, but what's the deal Frank?"

"Standard opening, novice," was the unwilling reply.

"Will you teach me how to play chess?"

"No." He then fell sound asleep at the table with his head cradled in his arms.

About one in the morning a young lieutenant burst through the door without knocking. He was the OD, or officer of the day, in charge of quarters for the night. He was an FNG. He stood in the doorway, seething, his eyes lashing out at all of us flopped out around the room, as if he expected us to jump to attention. "What are these women doing here?"

"Shining our boots and cleaning the barracks sir," Rick said.

He bristled like a porcupine. "Don't give me any of that soldier. Your asses are grass!" He stomped out and slammed the door behind him.

I got up and opened the door and stepped outside. I turned to Rick, who was still stretched out on the cot. "He's checking out all the rooms." He walked from room to room, chewing ass wherever there were women.

"Oh well, the new barracks probably needs another coat of paint," Rick chuckled.

In the morning we drove the girls back to town undisguised. The lieutenant stood in front of the TOC with his arms folded, eyeing us menacingly as we drove past.

The only people angry about it were the ones at the TOC. The SGM and the CO dutifully chewed us out, reminding us that a person had to have a top secret security clearance to get on post.

Nothing else came of it. Everybody knew that the officers in the TOC sneaked girl friends on post all the time, however discretely they did it.

Chapter 22

Continual Shadow

The reason our hooches were so new was not comforting. The year before, sappers got inside the compound with satchel charges. They managed to kick several doors in and throw in the explosive charges before they were killed.

If suicidal sappers managed to get inside a compound it was pure chaos. In our situation, since our indigenous team members carried AK's, and looked like VC anyway, it would be nearly impossible to tell friend from foe in the dark.

I slept with a .45 under my pillow every night, round chambered and pointed directly at the door.

Now Charlie dropped his mortars on us at night.

A siren was sounded and we all scrambled to a hasty formation, then ran to the sector of the perimeter we were to help defend.

The choppers got off the ground immediately, they were sitting ducks on the launch pads. The gunbirds circled the camp making gun runs, firing rockets and miniguns into the surrounding jungle. The miniguns poured a stream of red tracers that appeared as a solid band, raking to and fro, like a giant holding a bright red magic sword in the darkness. Many of the rounds ricocheted, splattering back into the air in all directions, like a molten red liquid thrown at the ground, splashing everywhere. I watched, fascinated at the spectacular sight.

Charlie walked his rounds methodically across the camp. The concussion conducted through the air felt as though it would break your eardrums and your body, jarring you to the bones. While the terror ripped through your soul, the shrapnel ripped through the air, tearing holes in buildings, vehicles, people, making ugly whistling noises in the air as the irregular shaped pieces of metal whipped above your head.

A lot of times Charley just set the tube up, dropped six or seven down the tube, then picked up the mortar and ran. The camp would be wide awake the rest of the night.

A mortar barrage puts the fear in anyone. The mortar rounds fall silently, you can't tell where they're coming from, and it's hard to know where the next one will hit.

The ever present question ran through everyone's minds during one of these attacks. "I wonder if the next one will get me."

There was the old adage, "You never hear the round that gets you."

Chapter 23

Painful Formation

I stood at the urinal in the latrine. A familiar fire coursed through my bladder and down my urethra. My knees buckled and I leaned against the wall for support. I forced myself to continue urinating, thinking, "No, not again." I was glad no one else was in the latrine to see the sweat appear on my flushed forehead. I left the latrine and headed straight for the dispensary.

Inside the dispensary was a line of Montagnard women and children waiting for medical attention. The scantily clad children sat on the concrete floor and played. There were several old women, a couple of mothers nursing infants.

Jerry looked up from his desk. "What are you up to, get over your dysentery OK?"

I nodded, trying to look nonchalant.

"What can we do for you?"

"I've got another problem this time."

"What is it?"

Probably not a single Yard in the waiting room spoke English, but I suddenly felt very self conscious. "Well," I hesitated.

"Have you got the clap again?" Jerry asked, grinning maliciously.

"Yeah."

"Come on." We went to a room in the back. He took a slide off the shelf and handed it to me. "Give me a smear." I did so and handed him the slide. He left the room, then came back with a bottle of tetracycline. "You better be thankful we've got tetracycline, penicillin doesn't work very well on this stuff you know."

I shook my head affirmatively.

"Where did you pick it up this time?" he asked.

"Same place," I said.

"Damn, this stuff just keeps popping up. I'll send somebody down there to check them out again. At least we've got them trained to wipe their asses from front to back."

"Maybe I'm just more susceptible to it, do you think," I asked.

"You're just unlucky, now get the hell out of here and be careful."

"Thanks." I left the dispensary.

When I came within sight of recon I saw that a formation was in progress. "Oh, no!" I mumbled, and ran toward Recon Company, but it was too late, they were dismissed. I'd missed the formation, had forgotten all about it when the fire hit in the latrine.

The sergeant major was standing in front of recon with his arms folded when I came running up.

"Well, Specialist Acre, did you decide you could fit our formation into your agenda after all? If I'd only known, we could have scheduled it more to your convenience."

"Sorry Sergeant Major, I was at the dispensary," I said, standing at parade rest.

"What was so important that it couldn't wait till after formation?"

"Well, I was in the latrine, when I started pissing fire, and all I could think about was getting to the medic," I said truthfully.

His severe features were carved in granite. I looked at the ground.

"How many times have you had the clap now Acre?" he finally asked.

"I don't know, four or five I think, Sergeant Major," I answered after some hesitation.

"Five times," he said. "Specialist Acre, do you know what this formation was for?" he asked sternly.

"No, I don't, Sergeant Major."

"I'll tell you what it was for, I announced the names of the specialist 4s who are going before the board in Pleiku next week to try to get their hard stripes." He looked me in the eyes like he was trying to see something inside my head. "Do you think your name was on that list?"

I looked at the ground some more. "I don't know Sergeant Major, I hope it was."

There was a long silence. I felt depressed.

Then he raised his clipboard and read the orders written on it. The orders listed the personnel who were to prepare for their oral examination in Pleiku, gave the time of the exam, the departing time and flight, and all the necessary details. He read the entire list of names. They were always alphabetical, and like most other military rosters that included me, my name was first on the list. He scrutinized me intensely.

"Somehow Specialist Drippy doesn't have the same ring to it that Sergeant Drippy does."

My heart rose from the pit into which it had been falling.

"Now get your ass over to your hooch and get ready to go to Pleiku. Dismissed!"

"Thank you Sergeant Major," I said, and headed for my hooch.

He called after me, "Study the manuals, Drippy!"

Chapter 24

Fate

It was July 1969 and I hadn't been away from Ban Me Thuot except for time in the field. The trip to Pleiku was a welcome respite. We all passed the boards. The questions were tough but I felt sure of myself and answered them easily. Questions concerning the rate of fire and maximum effective range of various weapons, questions about military discipline, communications. Mostly it was an intense inspection by the officers and senior ncos who constituted the board. Getting hard stripes was a major event, despite the fact that a buck sergeant was still the lowest ranking nco in Special Forces.

The fact that I came from MACV-SOG had a pronounced effect on the board. It was easy to feel confident. There were a couple of questions about the nature of our mission, which I felt obliged to answer with, "I'm not at liberty to answer that sir." Apparently it was the expected answer, for there was no attempt to pursue the question.

Back at BMT it was with pleasure and a sense of pride that the SGM handed us our orders telling us we'd been promoted. It felt great.

At about the same time, the astronauts were making their first moon landing. At night I stood looking at the sky, contemplating the fact that a man had actually stood on that hunk of green cheese and come back. It was stunning.

I told the SCU about it, pointing at the moon, telling them that America had put a man on the moon. At first they couldn't comprehend what I was trying to say, and after much effort, and many questions from my interpreter, I finally got the point across.

When he conveyed the information to the rest of the team, they looked at me skeptically with a sense of the ridiculous, and laughed, saying, "Beau coup dinky dau." Sure America has a man on the moon. America might have many wonders beyond their comprehension, but this was going too far, and I wasn't going to make fools of them.

This was the month that crazy Reich got an AK round in the chest and was sent to the hospital in Tokyo.

I was still not able to become inured to the fact that fate chose some to be wounded and some to die. It seemed so arbitrary, like the ducks that go by in an arcade at a carnival. A person shoots the BB gun at the targets zipping by, some get hit and fall, others make it across the field of fire.

Sometimes it seemed that a greater force had some effect on one's life and could preserve it, other times it seemed all left to chance, and one never knew which way the dice would fall.

When Reich came back we were all surprised and happy. We figured we'd never see him again. He didn't have to come back. He wanted to be back at Recon and practically had to go AWOL and get on a plane before they finally cut him orders to come back. He showed us his scar. The AK round hit a rib directly over his heart. The bullet followed the rib around the side of his chest and exited from the back underneath his left arm.

Whether by chance or act of providence, it was amazing to see proof that such things do happen, like the old story of the bullet that goes through the guy's helmet, spins around inside it, and comes to rest on top of his head.

Another incident just as incredible happened to the two Canadians in Recon. They got hit by enemy mortars just as the choppers were landing to exfil the team. A flying piece of steel hit Crimmings in the chest near his shoulder and knocked him into a bomb crater. While a couple of the other guys were dragging him toward the chopper, he thought it was all over, but when he finally got his wind back and felt his chest there was no sign of blood. He realized that he could move, got to his feet and raced for the chopper. Once in the air he stripped his shirt off, discovering a huge black and blue bruise forming on his chest. A piece of shrapnel had hit him flat and knocked the wind out of him and flipped him head over heels into the bomb crater, but he wasn't injured. If the piece of metal spinning through the air had hit in any other configuration it would likely have torn his chest open and embedded in a lung. If he'd been six inches closer or six

114

inches further away, the spinning, tumbling piece of shrapnel would have hit other than flatways.

Both of these men laughed it off, but it changed their lives.

Some men became more and more daring. Burkhart filled a sock with sand and stood behind a tree alongside a trail and waited for the last man to pass so he could hit him over the head with the sockful of sand, and take him prisoner. It never worked, the prisoner always wound up getting killed.

The other Canadian, Crimmings' partner, practiced diligently with a bow and arrow. He took this and an M-2 carbine to the field with intentions of taking a prisoner silently with the bow and arrow.

Hensley tried to convince our CO to let him go on a mission alone, but they wouldn't go for it. His motive for wanting to go it alone, I suspected, had something to do with the time he was along as the third American on a relatively new team. They'd been in the field for days, and the rest of the team took off their web gear for just a little while to alleviate the discomfort. Never taking off one's web gear, no matter how uncomfortable, was an iron clad rule. Charlie had them staked out, and as soon as they took off their web gear and started to eat something, Charlie ambushed them. The team had to run out of the ambush, Hensley was the only one who had his web gear on. Everybody else had only the magazine of ammo that was in their weapon. Luckily the choppers weren't far away, and they were able to reach a hill and get cover behind a pile of rocks, where Hensley laid down a base of fire while the choppers were on the way.

Taking a prisoner was highly desirable, in fact there were standing rewards for accomplishing it. We got a trip to Bangkok if we captured a POW. But capturing a prisoner was extremely difficult and full of complications, so many things could go wrong. Besides the fact that Charlie didn't want to be taken prisoner and often forced his would be captors to kill him, if the NVA knew a prisoner had been taken they would go to great lengths to get him back, sacrificing a lot of men to make sure the team didn't get out with the prisoner. They would pursue a team all day and all night anyway, and if the team had a prisoner, they had to move slower, and it became terribly dangerous. Then, if it was a Yard team, there was the ever present danger that the Yards would kill the prisoner before he got back. If the prisoner was wounded there was the likelihood that he would die before we got him back.

Several times the Yards killed a prisoner on the helicopter after the team had made it out safely. The Montagnards were liked and respected for the fine field soldiers they were, and there was no way to prevent them from killing a Vietnamese prisoner if they chose to do so. You don't threaten a Yard who's been in the field all his life and upon whom your life depends the next time you're in the field. They were offered rewards for bringing the prisoner back alive, but not many rewards were worth more than killing a Vietnamese.

The Yards struggle was with the Vietnamese. It was not for ideology or politics but for survival. They aligned themselves with us because we were fighting Vietnamese. The Montagnards were an oppressed people in Vietnam and were threatened with extinction. In their dealings with us they didn't lie or steal, and could never be accused of duplicity.

Frank had a Yard team. They had captured an NVA soldier and had him on the chopper headed for BMT. The prisoner was critically wounded and the medic was frantically trying to keep him alive. The prisoner died a few minutes before they got back to Ban Me Thuot.

After taking extraordinary risks to ambush and capture the soldier, Frank was so frustrated that he jumped onto the dying man's body, slapping his face and shouting, "If you die I'm going to kill you, you son of a bitch."

Chapter 25

No Substitute

Quan Loi was close to the Cambodian border. It was headquarters for the 1st Cavalry Airmobile, depicted in Frank Coppola's film "Apocalypse Now" by Robert Duvall as the archetypal 1st Cavalry commander who wore the cowboy hat and was the epitome of gladiator-like fearlessness.

Inside this compound was a small enclave, which was headquarters for our southernmost operations. It consisted of a small TOC, for the intelligence and operations personnel and the teletype, which maintained communications with BMT. There were several squad size tents for temporary quarters, a field mess tent, and a building about the size of a chicken coup, which served as our club while we were in Quan Loi.

The SCU were under strict orders to stay within our compound unless they were accompanied by an American team member. Some of the 1st Cavalry were pretty jumpy and trigger happy.

On this trip to Quan Loi we spent most of the first day monitoring a team in enemy contact. They were in the target adjoining the one we were to infiltrate.

They made contact with NVA just after sunrise and ran through dense jungle all morning. They ran for four hours, dropping smoke over their shoulders to mark their travel for the gunships, grenades with time delay fuses, CS grenades, claymores with time delays, everything they had, and still the NVA kept up the pursuit.

The gunships had to break away three times to go refuel and rearm. Cobra gunships were called in for support during the intervals. It was said that a cobra carried more armament than a B-17 bomber in World War II. But the NVA kept up the pursuit.

The bright light team was put on alert. Jim was on this one. The Cambodes and the three Americans waited in tense anticipation, checking every bit of communication that came in about the team.

"What do you think Jim, you still want to run recon?" I asked.

"Of course," he snapped. "I never get to the field except on locals or on bright light."

"Yeah, but we need you," I said. "That's when the shit is really flying."

"I still want to run recon," he said bitterly.

"Well, good luck if you have to go in."

"Thanks, the way it looks we'll need it."

I didn't relish his job. If the team got pushed into a position in which they couldn't move and were in trouble, Jim would have to lead the Cambodes, who were fierce fighters, into the firefight and get with the recon team to give ground support. The other situation was unthinkable, they'd have to go in and get the bodies if the team was wiped out.

A cheer went up. The team had made it to an area with sufficient clear space for the choppers to be able to drop the ropes down far enough to pull them out. Then we heard one American was wounded, which sobered everybody immediately.

We headed for the chopper pads to wait. In a half hour we could see them in the distance. Seven choppers: four gunships, two slicks, and the medevac. Clumps could be seen dangling from one of the slicks at the ends of long strings. Then, as the choppers came closer, those clumps turned into men hanging from hundred-foot ropes.

The slick with the men on the ropes hovered high above the compound and slowly descended until their feet touched the ground and they released themselves and ran for the edge of the chopper pad.

We rushed forward with cans of beer in outstretched hands.

The medic was already checking out the hand of one of the Americans. He held up his hand, there was a hole completely through it. The round had passed through his hand, hadn't hurt a tendon or hit a vein or artery. He wouldn't have the use of the hand for a while, but later after the doctors x-rayed it he was assured that it would be OK.

The XO happened to be at Quan Loi for an aerial recon in the new C&C chopper. He immediately insisted that the team get their gear ready and go right back in. The team refused. He was adamant.

"But sir, we just came out on the ropes after running half the day, everybody is exhausted," the team leader protested.

"I rode the ropes back at Ban Me Thuot, it's not that big a deal," the XO said.

The team leader pointed out that riding the ropes back at BMT was fun, like a carnival ride, this was different, besides, his radio operator was wounded.

The XO said the third American on the team could carry the radio.

The one-zero said he wasn't going back in.

The XO said, "I'll have you court martialed."

The team leader declared, "Fine, court martial me," and stomped away.

The team leader won, though not making his relations any better with the XO.

The team leader made the final decision about any mission, besides the missions were strictly volunteer and a man couldn't be court martialed for refusing to go.

The XO fumed and ranted and confirmed that he was an ass hole, but knew he'd lost.

After dinner I wandered over to the crew chiefs' hooches. I stepped up on the wooden platform, parted the tent flaps and stuck my head inside. "Paul, you here?"

"Come on in, good to see you," he waved a sun tanned arm to me.

"Just wondered how it goes with the easy money around here," I said, stepping inside.

"Yeah, easy money my ass, you should have seen us today, I just about burnt up the barrel on my sixty."

"I believe it, you know I wouldn't trade you jobs for all the money in the world," I said.

He smiled, "The feeling's mutual, you couldn't get me off my chopper to go running around in that fucking jungle." His blonde hair was sun bleached white and contrasted with the deep tan of his face and torso. "Have a seat," he motioned to the wooden rocket crate that served as a stool beside his cot. He looked at my name tag, "Were you related to that major that was in the C&C chopper that went down?"

I looked at my name tag. "No, not that I know of, we didn't really have a chance to get acquainted."

"Well, it's kind of an uncommon name, I just wondered," he said.

"He's the first person I ever met who spelled his name just the same who wasn't related to me," I said. I looked again at the embroidered name tag on my chest.

"It was a bad deal all the way around," he said quietly.

"Where did you go for R&R?" I asked, trying to change the subject.

He hesitated a moment, then said, "Sydney."

"Good times huh? Everybody says the Round Eyes are great in Sydney." Sydney was the place everybody wanted to go for R&R.

"You gone on R&R yet?" He looked disturbed.

"No, not yet. What's the matter Paul, wasn't Sydney any good?"

"Oh, it was fine, fine," he said, nodding his head and looking at the floor. "Here, want to light this?" He held out a joint. I lit it, took a hit and handed it back. "It was just strange, really weird."

"All I've heard is great stories about all the fantastic women in Sydney," I said.

"You should hear about my R&R," he handed the joint to me.

"OK, lets hear it," I said, drawing the smoke in.

He rubbed his temples with his fingertips, then looked at me, "You really want to hear about it?"

"You want to talk about it, I want to hear it." I felt the smoke opening up my head.

"OK. You know I had a year in country and I extended, so I decided to go to Sydney for thirty days. Like you say, the place everybody wants to go. Well, I got to Sydney and met a girl in a bar, like everybody else. She invited me over to her place. We got to talking and it turns out she's interested in the occult and witchcraft and stuff like that, then she finally tells me she's a witch and wants to know if I'd like to come to a seance she's having."

"What did she look like?" I interjected.

"She was dark headed, sort of a dark brunette, about five nine, really good looking, nice body, long straight hair. I thought she was beautiful. Anyway, I said sure, I'd go to her seance if she wanted. I didn't know anything about that stuff, sounded strange to me, but I figured if she was willing to spend time with me, and I'm just out of the field in Nam, I could go to her stupid seance, you know.

"Anyway, we wound up at her dining room table with a bunch of other people I'd never seen before. She had a candle on the center of the table, it was the only light in the room. She told everybody to hold hands, then she would call on the spirit world. I was getting a kick out of it, kind of. She started saying a bunch of stuff I don't remember, kind of like a prayer, when all of a sudden she got real afraid sounding, and said, 'Someone at this table has powers,' and she looked right at me. Then she got up and ran out of the room. Well, we didn't know what to do. One of her friends went in the bedroom to see about her. Finally everybody sort of drifted away and went home or whatever. I didn't know what to do. She never came out of the bedroom, so I finally left."

Paul was wide eyed now, telling the story with expression and gesturing with his hands. "I went outside and was walking down the street when a blonde girl stopped me. She pulled me over under a street light and showed me a picture of Jesus. She held it in front of me and said to watch the eyes open and close. Sure enough the eyes of Jesus opened and closed. She said, 'Monique is a black witch and she is going to try to steal your powers.' I said 'Powers? What powers? What the hell are you talking about?'

"She asked me to come over to her place and she'd tell me all about it. So I went over to her place, where she played her guitar for me and sang beautiful songs. You just wouldn't believe how beautiful she could play the guitar and sing. After she sang some songs I felt better, and asked her what she had meant when she'd told me Monique was going to try and steal my powers.

"She said, 'You're a warlock and you have powers, whether you realize it or not. Monique knows it and will try to steal them from you.'

"'How can she steal powers from me that I don't even know I have?' I wanted to know. And I wanted to know about her and why she was talking like that.

"She said she practiced white magic, that her master was good, and that she had been sent to warn me that my life was in danger. She told me about a GI that Monique had put a curse on and had made the car he'd rented pull to the side under its own power and run off a bridge, killing the guy. This was all too fuckin much.

"After spending the evening with her I went back to my hotel room and thought about it all. I decided to go back over to Monique's."

"God, why did you do that?" I asked.

"I was curious," he answered, "You know, it was all too much not to check into."

"I guess so," I nodded.

"Anyway, the next day I went back to Monique's. She was glad to see me and apologized for running away like that. I asked her if she thought I was a warlock and she said she knew I was. She told me a lot of stuff about herself. One thing she said was that her spirit would come to take her at an early age. She said it like it made her sad."

"Her spirit would come to take her?" I questioned.

"Something about the spirit she served would take her as part of the price of the powers she enjoyed on earth," he answered.

I felt a chill down my spine as he told the story. There was no insincerity in his face. I forgot about the punch line, for which I had been waiting at first. He held the joint out to me, I shook my head, declining any more, "I've got to go to the field tomorrow."

He took a long toke. "By this time I was so intrigued by the whole thing that I said I'd go when she invited me to a party at a hotel. We went to the party and it was about like any other party you've been to, people drinking and getting high and talking and joking. We'd been there a couple of hours when Monique came running out of the bathroom screaming, 'He's coming too soon, he's coming too soon!' I mean she was hysterical. Some woman and another guy and me went into the bathroom to see what she was running from."

His eyes were huge and he was shaking, "Well, in the bathroom the mirror was bleeding!"

"What?" I said. "What do you mean the mirror was bleeding?"

"That's right," he nodded his head repeatedly, "The mirror was bleeding. It was running out of four letters spelled on the mirror, running down the mirror and in the sink and on the floor. There was at least a quart of blood before it finally quit."

"What were the letters?" I asked.

"They were c, o, l, l," he said apprehensively.

"C, o, l, l," I repeated, "I wonder what that could have meant."

"I don't know, but we cleaned up the bathroom after it quit, and we opened the medicine cabinet and checked it out real good and there was no sign of anything unusual about it."

"That is weird, I mean really weird," I said. "It's scary, what did you do then?"

"I left Australia two weeks early and came back here, I was so freaked out."

"God, I don't blame you, that was really strange."

"The story isn't over yet," he said. "I came back here and just laid around for the next two weeks. I built the place up a little." He pointed to the wooden wall around the inside of the tent, built out of mortar crates and rocket crates, a kind of war-zone wainscot. He'd also built shelves along the walls. Some of the pieces of wood had stenciling on them, "81mm mortar," "white phosphorous," "HE."

"It looks good, you made it pretty nice for everybody," I said, meaning it.

"Well, I had the time, it was kind of fun," he said. "Anyway, when it came time for me to go back on duty I went back to flying again. We were waiting at the launch site at Bu Dop for you guys, just sitting around bullshitting, when I told this same story to my pilot and copilot. We were leaning up against the front of the chopper, and when I came to the part about the mirror bleeding, I drew the letters in the dust on the nose of the chopper like so," he drew the letters in the air with his forefinger, "then I wiped it out again. We came back to Quan Loi that night, and when we got here the CO told our pilot that they were going to use our slick for the C&C chopper the next day. I hung around the chopper and cleaned it up a little, since the brass would be in it, rearmed everything, you know, the crew chief always gets the chopper ready for the next day. Anyway, I was working on it, when I got the funniest feeling, got all scared, and I all of a sudden decided I couldn't fly any more. I finished prepping the chopper and went straight to the CO and told him I didn't want to fly any more. You know, after a year's flying, you can quit crewing if you want to and they'll give you duty on post. He said OK, they'd send somebody else to crew the C&C AR the next day." The color had drained from his face, despite the suntan it was almost white. He faltered, wiped at a spot on the floor with his shoe. "The next day that chopper was shot down, it was the C&C chopper." His eyes were full of tears and his voice shook with emotion.

My blood froze as the cold chill went up and down my spine and settled in my stomach.

"After that happened, I went back to flying, I decided nobody was ever going in my place again. If it's my time, it's my time."

I wondered if my face was as white as his. I didn't mention anything about to whom my fatigues had belonged. He didn't need to hear that. I didn't need to hear that.

"That's got to be the spookiest story I've ever heard, what do you think it means?"

"Hell, I don't know, all I know is, nobody will ever go in my place again!"

Chapter 26

The Graduate

After hearing Paul's story I withdrew to the "chicken coup" club to order a drink. Narrow shafts of light streamed out through the cracks in the makeshift building. Inside, beneath two bare light bulbs, stood White, the minigun red baron, washing whiskey glasses. He worked in the communications center and tended the bar at night. He set up a whiskey and coke, "How'd you get hooked into going to the field with M_____ and S_____?" He looked concerned.

"Ah, they've both been wanting to run recon for several months, I don't know what happened really," I said.

M_____ was a communications Sergeant who had been assigned to our unit from a conventional unit up north. He'd been working in the commo shack at BMT. He had a lot of tales to tell about combat missions in the notorious A Shau Valley and had a propensity to shoot his mouth off. He'd been badgering the people in command to assign him to recon. S_____ was the supply sergeant for B-50, and also had the idea that he wanted to run recon. M was a sergeant first class, and S was a staff sergeant. They both qualified in my book as lifers, not professional soldiers. At any rate they had both finally gotten their wish and had been assigned to a recon mission. We were short of men during this time, because there were more and more missions. There was the feeling in the air and word on the grapevine that something was going to happen before long, nobody knew exactly what, but something was in the mill. (That something was the invasion of Cambodia, which President Nixon announced on nationwide television early in 1970.)

White wiped the bar top with a sponge. "They went to Kontum for one-zero school didn't they?"

"Oh yeah, they just got back, this is their first mission," I said.

"Oh Christ, an arc light for their first mission," he shook his head. "You've been on an arc light haven't you?"

"Nope."

"Well, just hope like hell that you get in and out before Charlie does," he said gravely, his face was intense. He was dipping glasses in soapy water.

"You bet."

"You know, the last arc light I went on, they were all so dazed, the ones that were alive, Charlie was just wandering around the place disoriented, some of them were numb and blinded, like they were just rendered insensible by the concussion. We got in and out without a problem. That was the one mission I was on that we got a POW. We were lucky, it was almost easy." He dried the glasses and set them behind the bar on a rack made from a mortar crate.

"That's good, maybe we'll be as lucky."

"Still sounds like a fuck-up to me, keep an eye on those two. When you going in?" he asked.

"Tentatively day after tomorrow, the VR is in the morning." I finished off the drink and slid the glass toward him.

"The movie's in a half hour," he said, setting up another drink.

"Great," I said, "What is it?"

"'The Graduate,' have you seen it?"

I smiled. "Yeah, I've seen it, been in love with Katherine Ross ever since."

"You and the whole United States Army," he laughed.

"At least." I sipped the drink, watched him dry the glasses, thought about Paul's story, thought about the two Americans I was going to the field with. "Think we should have gotten into plastics instead of guerrilla warfare?"

"We've got plastic explosives, the best of both worlds," he raised his hands, palms up, grinning and rolling his eyes.

"That's bad, that's really bad!"

The movie screen and projector were set up outdoors, in the middle of the compound beside the "chicken coup" club. We brought all the chairs out from the TOC and set them in rows in front of the sheet that served as a screen.

It seemed incongruous seeing "The Graduate" again; the juxtaposition between the theatre at Wichita while I was in college, and the setting at Quan Loi, with mortar and artillery rounds going off constantly in the distance, the illumination rounds casting ghostly yellow light. The movie up on the screen, serving some strange connection between the two realities. I felt odd and hollow and lonely.

I left my seat midway in the movie and plodded over to the solitary tree that had somehow managed to survive in the middle of the compound. I visited with my SCU team members, who were gathered around the tree. I passed Salems out to everybody and we talked in pigeon English about the wonders of Da Lat and the day we would all go there. We talked about the upcoming mission.

Bo sat next to me and spoke quietly in his halted English. He was Chinese Vietnamese, about my age. He had a wispy moustache, which he trimmed periodically. "You, thing maybe someday, I learn English good, may-be (he stretched the word out in two long syllables) I go United State?" I thought I saw a hint of pleading in his face, which was lit dimly in the dancing light of the movie behind us.

I didn't know what to say. I knew the odds were slim that he could ever go to the States. "I don't know, Bo, maybe you could. Maybe I won't go back to the States."

"You, you, stay Vietnam maybe one year, maybe two year, then you go home. Me, me stay Vietnam, war, only war."

The SCU didn't talk like this very often. There was little comfort I could give. I had given my team things like a transistor radio for their barracks at BMT, for which they'd have had to save a long time. I gave them C rations and American cigarettes and other things that were expensive for them or difficult to obtain. Little compensation for the dedication and protection they offered me in the field. But I didn't have much to offer their doubts and uncertainties. I found that, though they were "mercenaries," they were really just young guys about my age who took the best job they could find, who had the courage to dress like NVA and go into Cambodia with a couple of Americans. I had to appreciate the irony that this was their way of avoiding the draft in their country.

"Maybe there will be peace, Bo," I said.

He snorted and shook his head, "No." We sat silently.

I pulled my lighter from my pocket and lit a cigarette. I looked at the lighter in the dim flickering light. I read the inscription. CCS, Acre, 1969. I read the other side, onto which I'd had engraved the saying about life having a flavor the protected will never know. "Here Bo, take this, I want you to have it, you're a better man than you know."

He took the lighter hesitatingly, then looked at it. "What say?" He pointed to the inscription on the back.

"Have Tai translate it for you," I said, and headed for the tent.

Chapter 27

VR

B y first light the C&C chopper was headed for the area marked for destruction by the B-52 strike. The sun rose reluctantly, lighting the fog laden jungle with increasing rays that first stretched toward us, then passed by into the darkness in the west. Opaque mists hung in the hollows; on the hilltops trees poked through the fog.

After we'd been in the air for nearly thirty minutes, the fog had mostly dissipated. Suddenly the chopper descended from cruising altitude and raced close to the treetops, above a primitive scene of bamboo and underbrush, spaced with clumps of trees. Underneath the foliage I could make out grass hooches, trails, open areas, stacks of supplies, everything but people. When they heard the sound of the chopper they disappeared. I readied my weapon in case we took fire. There was no human discernible on the ground.

I wondered why they chose not to fire on us. We were nearly thirty minutes flight inside Cambodia, which at 75 knots was over thirty miles. For whatever reasons, there was no sign of life below, other than the obvious fact that someone was living there.

After we'd overflown the area for fifteen or twenty minutes, the chopper headed back for Quan Loi.

On the way back I considered the fact that the choppers were thirty minutes from the target, further than average. That meant a minimum of thirty minutes reaction time from the moment I established contact with the FAC pilot. On an arc light we would have constant contact with a FAC pilot. This mission was intended for one day only, an assessment of damages, for as long as we could make it last.

I thought about the peculiar machinations of the military that were putting me in the field on an arc light with two guys on their first missions. The one was an E-7, and had, if he told the truth, considerable combat experience. The other, an E-6, was mainly wanting his combat infantryman's badge, I suspected, and would be in and out of recon in a hurry.

An arc welder emits a light so bright that it will instantly burn unprotected eyes. When the welding rod comes close to the metal, the resulting heat from the electric arc liquefies both the rod and the object being welded, fusing them into a solid piece. Hence, I assumed, the apt name arc light for a bombing by B-52s.

Many times I had heard the B-52s overhead in the night, many times I'd heard the destructive inferno in the distance, felt the earthquake it created, watched the lightening storm above the jungle.

Back at Quan Loi the intelligence and operations officers finished briefing us. The primary objective was to get into the area as quickly as possible after the bombing, examine the destruction, find whatever intelligence material was available, anything from papers found on bodies to files in destroyed hooches. We were being inserted directly on top of what was reported to be a Battalion headquarters. Taking a live prisoner was always the most desirable thing.

The main thing was to get in and out before Charlie did. Charlie would be rushing in medical help, his own damage report teams, and combat troops.

Of all the tales about recon infiltrations, the most gruesome were recons of arc lights. Stories about mangled bodies blown beyond recognition, pieces of bodies scattered around like discarded meat, blind, bleeding, and disoriented soldiers wandering around in a daze, while the recon team walked in and surveyed the damage, took what they wanted, and left.

There were also tales of recon teams being hit from several sides by the onrush of angry troops. More than one team had been lost on an arc light recon.

There was not much rest in my sleep that night. Thoughts competing for attention circled like buzzards in my imagination.

One image bought a semblance of sleep. I had the radio and the SCU.

Chapter 28

Recon an Arc Light

At dawn the chopper left us on a little flat spot next to a twenty-foot bomb crater. The smell of explosives was strong, hanging in the air like death. The one thousand pound bomb had blown a ton or more of earth away, laying the surrounding bamboo over like spokes in a wheel around the resulting crater. In every direction I saw bomb craters everywhere. Four inch bamboo was laid horizontally around each crater, held up three feet from the ground by the underbrush.

M_____, the team leader, was confused. We huddled against an undamaged stand of brush while he fumbled with his map and compass. His hands were shaking uncontrollably. He couldn't find our location on the map. S_____, the E-6, crouched near him looking helpless. They both looked at me apprehensively. The SCU gave me looks of disgust. This was worse than I had imagined.

I took the map, placed it on the ground, oriented it to north, showed M_____ the location of our insertion, then held my compass up, pointing out the azimuth we were to take.

After a few minutes M_____ seemed to regain his composure somewhat. I pointed in the direction we were to move. He shook his head affirmatively. We got up to proceed.

I couldn't believe how difficult it was to progress, even if moving silently hadn't been necessary. The blown over bamboo was too high to step over easily, it was too low to crawl underneath without getting hung up in the underbrush or on the bamboo. The slightest hit of something hard and the bamboo would send a signal like castanets through the silence. Walking down into and back up out of the craters wasn't practical. Walking around the edge of each crater was about the only choice, then try to worm a path through the downed bamboo that had fallen in the general direction we wanted to go.

For two hours we crept slowly ahead in single file, stopping, looking, listening. We'd moved only three hundred meters when we came into a small area that was less devastated. I quietly sighed relief. This would be better cover for a while, at least enough to catch my wits.

We were barely into this area when to my right I saw an NVA soldier walking toward us. I stared in horror-stricken fascination. He wasn't wounded or semiconscious or staggering around in a daze. He was dressed in clean olive drab fatigues, and had a steel helmet with a chin strap. The fatigues looked freshly starched and pressed.

He didn't see us. He was directly opposite me, ten meters away, walking and peering in the direction from which we'd just come.

I thought momentarily about a POW, then dismissed it quickly. Something was wrong. The sharp cracks of my CAR-15 exploded the silence and the NVA disappeared from view. At the moment I opened up, the rest of the team opened up in the same direction, and at the next split second a B-40 exploded close to S_____, and AK rounds were tearing the branches off the shrubs around us. According to standard procedure for the radio man, I ran perpendicularly to the team, away from the direction of fire, to a point about fifteen meters away. From here I covered the back of the team, and attempted to establish radio contact with the FAC. I couldn't raise anybody.

For several minutes the team poured all its firepower into the jungle in the direction of the enemy. S_____ had taken a hit from the B-40 that landed near him and was bleeding from the thigh. He was lucky that the B-40 had hit beside him and not in front of him, he wouldn't have had any legs to worry about. Most of Charlie's B-40's had a shaped charge designed for armor, which directs most of the force straight ahead for penetration. However, the leg wound was bleeding badly and needed immediate attention.

M_____, the team leader was completely out of control, shaking, and had followed me to my position instead of directing the team's fire.

The SCU and S_____ quit firing and waited. There was no fire coming back.

"Now what," I thought. I assumed Charlie would start advancing toward us from two directions, or attempt to set up another ambush.

S_____ looked over his shoulder at me, I motioned for him to join us. He limped over to us. I told S_____ to sit down, and had M_____ cut open the leg of his pants and tend his wounds. I put the SCU in defensive positions around us while S_____ was getting patched up and I tried to get somebody on the radio again. Still no response.

"Can you walk?" I whispered to S_____. I looked at the ugly rips in his leg, which M_____ pulled shut, wrapping gauze around the leg.

"Yeah," he grimaced.

The mind has a way of working on automatic in situations like this. I was practically a disinterested observer of my own logic, as I decided that our best bet was to return the way we had come. Ordinarily this would not be a good decision, but in this circumstance it seemed the thing to do. We knew the direction we had come. We didn't know anything about any other heading, except any other heading should lead deeper into the base camp.

There was a burst of gunfire from one of the SCU. I rushed up beside him.

"VC, go over," he pointed, making an arc with his forefinger extended.

"They're trying to get behind us," I thought.

"Come on," I whispered, indicating that we should move out.

We moved as fast as we could away from the point of contact.

We found a bomb crater that looked good and clambered into it, circling around the inside to defend in all directions.

"Now if they just don't have any mortars," I thought. I tried the radio again. Nothing. "Should we try to run? Shit, if this is a battalion base camp, there's no telling what we'll run in to. But they may be trying to get around us now. It may take them awhile to find us, maybe they won't suspect that we back tracked. Yeah, right."

"Wasp this is Spider," I tried the radio again.

"Spider this is Wasp, go ahead." I felt a wave of relief.

"Roger, I have team in contact, one man wounded." I gave the code words for these terms.

"Roger, understand team in contact, one man wounded, the choppers are in the air," came the reply.

The jungle was quiet. I peered into the array of plant life, trying to see just one foot further. Seconds were like minutes, minutes were like hours.

"Spider, this is Wasp, we're under attack ourselves, get back to you in a minute."

"Roger." I wondered what the hell that was supposed to mean.

Twenty more minutes and the gunships were strafing the jungle around us. Toward the direction we'd made contact the sound of AK's firing could be heard as the gunbird passed overhead.

"Wasp, you're taking fire on your pass, azimuth 30."

"Roger."

They made three more passes. After the third pass there was no more fire.

The medevac chopper dropped into the clearing while the jungle burst into chaos around us. On the way out the SCU's faces were grim. They said nothing to the other two Americans.

The choppers had been under attack by some A1Es with Vietnamese pilots who were roaming around. Since they were on the wrong side of the border the A1Es had opened up on them. It had taken some time to get on the radio and make contact and explain why the choppers were there.

The major in charge of the mission was given a reprimand for pulling the FAC away from us and sending him to another area for a VR. On an arc light, the recon team was supposed to have constant radio contact.

"Sergeant Acre reporting sir," I saluted and stood at attention.

"At ease," the captain returned my salute. "You didn't have a chance to see much in there did you?"

"No sir."

"Too bad Charlie got help in there so fast."

"Yes sir."

"Do you think M_____ will make a team leader?"

"Well, sir, he's a senior nco and I don't think it's my place to say anything."

He studied my face a minute. "Do you want to go to the field with him again?"

"No sir."

"Who should I put with him?"

"I don't know sir, I wouldn't want any of my friends to go."

"OK, that's all I wanted, go relax awhile, you're dismissed."

"Thank you sir." I saluted, did an about face and left recon headquarters.

M_____ didn't run any more recon missions. He went back to work in the commo shack. S_____ was in the hospital for a couple of weeks. He didn't come back to CCS. He got a job as liaison in Nha Trang.

Chapter 29

Nightmare

It was a lazy morning. After checking the duty roster, I leaned against the rail in front of recon company, lit a cigarette, and pondered the only mistake the commander from West Point had made. At the end of one row of hooches was a set of platforms, staggered from fifteen feet high, to ten feet, to five feet. Ropes with knots tied at one foot intervals hung from the highest platform. It was an obstacle course. In the evenings when the weather was nice we used the highest platform to sit and smoke a joint and watch the sun go down.

Concluding that it really wasn't a mistake after all, I saw, over the top of the obstacle course, a slick in the distance. As it approached I noticed something unusual about it. One person was riding the ropes. As the slick got closer I could see that it was an American. When it got even closer I threw my cigarette to the ground and ran for the chopper pads.

The rope was tied, instead of to a Swiss seat or web gear, in a loop underneath his arms, which hung limply. His head was hanging back, rolling with the motion of the chopper. The crew chief was looking down over the skids, directing the pilot's descent.

When I got to the chopper pad the slick was directly above me, lowering the limp body to the ground. His head lay sideways, motionless. When his feet touched the ground, he made no effort to stand. I grabbed the big man under the arms and lowered him to the ground onto his back, then untied the rope.

The medic's jeep screeched to a halt beside us, the medic jumped out and started administering first aid.

I stepped back to give him room. The face was white, lifeless, unrecognizable. And it finally registered.

"It's Jim!" The realization struck without warning. My knees buckled. I sat on the ground.

The medic worked frantically.

By this time others, including Jim's first sergeant, had gathered on the chopper pads. My head was swimming.

One medic was giving artificial respiration, the other medic started CPR. He checked again for a pulse. They worked on him for a long time. Finally they both shook their heads silently, kneeling beside the lifeless form. "He was already gone in the air," one of them whispered.

I didn't stay and watch them carry him away. I was lost in a swirling sea, hearing Jim tell me from across an incorporeal table, to go see his folks, go see his girlfriend, have his dad name that damn bull after him.

I slammed the door and dropped to the cot. The rest of the day and evening were a blur.

That night, I found myself outside, leaning against the wall of a hooch, talking to Rick.

"Remember the FTX (field training exercise) at Ft. Bragg?" I asked.

"The torture test?" Rick nodded. "I've never been so hungry. I remember that poor persimmon tree that we stripped clean, and when you guys low crawled all night."

"Uh huh, I can still hear Jim screaming, 'No sergeant, I'll never quit.'" We were laughing through tears. A distant illumination round faintly lit Rick's face.

"And the whole company stood there on our knees with our weapons held out," he held his arms in front of him, "and our packs on our backs." He wiped his sleeve across his face.

Our company had been without sleep for days, with hardly any food, except for a few potatoes and onions, and a goat they gave us and made us slaughter and make jerky. Four of us were on night listening post, when the company was ordered to move out. The company stumbled away in a trance without us. When the cadre found us asleep in the mud, they gave a "special class" for the "fuckups." The company stood all night on their knees with weapons held out at arms length, packs on their backs, watching the four of us crawl back and forth from the river, where we were forced to dunk over our heads, packs, weapons and all, then low crawl to the obstacle course, run through it yelling at the top of our lungs, then low crawl back to the river for another dunking. The cadre screamed at us, berating us constantly, then they'd tell us quietly and sympathetically, "You can have a hot shower and a hot meal, and sleep in a warm bunk, all you have to do is quit, come on give up, you'll never make it."

Jim was the most determined of all. His tortured voice echoed through the forest, "No Sergeant, I'll never quit, you can't make me quit!"

"That's what I can't understand," I mused, "he was the most determined, the most emphatic of all of us. Did he sense something inevitable about his fate."

"What are you talking about?" Rick asked.

"You know that evening Jim was bummed out, well, I didn't tell you what he was bummed out about. He knew he was going to die."

"How's that?" Rick said softly.

"He told me to have his dad name a bull after him, to go see his family and his girlfriend. I tried to get him to think differently, but he wouldn't hear it, just insisted that I promise to do it."

"Whew," was Rick's response.

"This is really weird, this has really got me crazy, I mean, after that conversation, and then I'm leaning against the rail over there and I see the chopper come in and I'm the first one to get to him." The emotions rolled through me in a buffeting tide.

Rick's team leader carried a Bible all the time. He came over and read some things from it, but it didn't do much good. I was in a place where nothing was going to reach me.

Bill was probably Jim's best friend. He was grieved and angry. He wanted to know what had happened. Why they'd sent him back tied on the ropes like that.

The whole of recon company was awash with grief and anger.

I wandered around the post till late in the night. I didn't drink or smoke anything, just sat out on the berm, and walked around aimlessly.

Long after midnight, when I got back to the hooch, Rick and Deak were in bed asleep. I wearily climbed into the bunk to see if I could sleep. I was drifting into sleep fitfully, when a point of light appeared in the air beside my cot. I watched it grow larger. I screamed.

Deak jumped from his cot and put his hand on my arm. "It's OK," he said.

"I saw something, something forming in the air beside my cot, it was Jim," I sobbed.

"Well it's all right now, just try to get some sleep."

"OK." I lay awake trembling, finally drifting into sleep, telling Jim that I'd keep the promise.

Chapter 30

Reverie and Poetry

At night we sometimes smoked the joints that the mamason at the laundry furnished us. One had to admire such resourcefulness and persistence. Her young helpers very carefully rolled cigarettes between their hands, removing the tobacco. The empty tubes were painstakingly stuffed with the potent cannabis, then replaced in the package just as carefully, with even the cellophane restored. One could buy whatever brand of cigarette he smoked. I smoked Marlboros. In the left breast pocket, regular cigarettes, in the right, the special ones. Smoking through the filter made the smoke mellow.

"You want a sip?" Rick held out the brown bottle.

I took the bottle, removed the loose cork, and sipped the sweet liquid. "You think we could get the girls on post again?" The drink was Obesitol, a French weight reducer Rick had found downtown at the drug store. It tasted like cough syrup. The label was a silly cartoon of an obese man with spindly legs and a huge gut hanging over his shorts.

"Why bother? They'll hide us out downtown."

"Yeah, that's right."

"How are you and fat Felds getting along?" Fat Felds was an E-6 lifer who'd just come to recon, full of stories about having run recon since the Projects started.

I scowled. "As well as I get along with any lifer ass hole. You know what really bothers me?"

"What really bothers you?"

"I can't carry him."

"You can't carry him?"

"Yeah, if he catches a round, there's no way I could carry him, I don't think two of us could carry him. So what the fuck do I do, leave him?" In the field his puffy face turned beet red, the sweat cascading in streams.

"You get your MPC exchanged?" Rick was threading a different tape onto the recorder.

"I didn't have much money left this month to worry about."

"You heard what Becktoldt did today."

"No, what'd he do?"

"He called the MPs and told them there was an E-8 downtown with a load of piasters and MPC."

"You're kidding! That's great, that's just super, what happened?"

An E-8 lifer at the TOC had made life miserable for us. He'd tried to organize inspections, tried to get recon included in a bunch of detail work, tried to get us under his thumb. Periodically there was a change in military payment certificates. On a given day, all MPC had to be exchanged for the new, all the old was voided, no longer viable currency. It was supposed to be a surprise, to discourage blackmarket profiteering.

"Nobody knows for sure," Rick curled his lip and raised his eyebrows in an ironic smile. "After the money exchange, those guys saw him head for town carrying a couple of suspicious looking bags, so they just called the MPs. Haven't heard anything."

"I hope they nailed his ass."

What the E-8 could have done was go downtown and buy up all the available MPC from the black market at less than fifty cents on the dollar, then come back and exchange it for the new MPC, making a healthy profit. Since he was in charge of the MPC exchange, it would be easy for him to fix the books.

I took a new ten dollar MPC bill from my wallet. "Like to have the job of designing these things, this one's got a guy with a beret, you notice that?"

"Yeah, look at the rifle."

I studied the bill. It was similar to U.S. currency, except it was smaller, and had several colors. In the center, instead of Washington or Lincoln, was a picture of a soldier. "I'll be damned!" I laughed and laughed. The picture was indeed a soldier with a beret, with a jungle background, obviously a Vietnam setting. He was holding an M-14, which we didn't use, but the distinctive thing about the picture was the blank adapter on the end of the M-14. When garrison Army was playing war games, the soldiers shot blanks, and in order for the rifle to eject the spent cartridge and load a new one, a blank adapter had to be put over the end of the muzzle. "A fucking blank adapter, that's got to be some Army artist's idea of a joke." I was still laughing.

"They probably contracted all the art work to some private firm," Rick offered.

"I'd rather think it was a statement of some kind," I said.

"Depends on who did it."

"Yeah."

It was late, well past midnight. The camp was quiet. Rick got out his little bottles of paint and was painting an intricate multicolored flower on the wall. I relaxed in a luxurious sea of color and sound. I felt a familiar nudging, found my pen and notebook and started writing.

"What are you so engrossed in?" Rick asked, looking up from his flower.

"That's really an outrageous flower," I said, ignoring the question.

"Come on, that's a diary, you know you can't keep a fucking diary."

"Fuck you."

"Let me see it."

"No, besides, it's not a diary."

"Then if it's not a diary, let me see what you're writing, I let you see my flower." He was smiling.

"You'll just laugh at me."

"So? No I won't laugh, let me see."

I threw the notebook to him. He opened it and read aloud.

In some of my deepest moments
A never dying ember glows through.
The trace, though slight, remains to remind.
Though long forgotten and assumed
All repaired, the stairs still
Show what once came that way.

It's been these slight reminders
That have shown the imprint
Though not the stamp was permanent.
Though reshelved deep

141

In seldom used sources
It's made its mark
And cannot be erased.

Daylight Moonlight Night, I know
The paints flaking in my mind.
Gears once meshed and turning
Are grating and grinding.

The pretty picture formed inside
Hardly resembles the hard reality.
Nothing is as it seems it should be.

Good and Bad, Right and Wrong
A Son sent to answer all the questions
So easy to mold inside a
Newcomers eager, thirsty thoughts.

A beautiful, innocent child.
The child surpasses the teachers
So quickly, so sadly thrust
Into turmoil.

The Definitions fade into nothingness,
Suddenly grasping, searching, frenzied,
The lost shadow begs not forget.

The Search begins
There to where we cannot know,
For the real answers, if discovered
Are beyond us, as a hand
Grasping to hold light.

He handed the book back to me and picked up his brush. His face was intent on the complex design. I looked for some clue to his thoughts.

"You're not laughing."

"No."

"Well?"

"Well what?" He was outlining the contours of the flower with a thin black line.

"What do you think?"

"I'm curious."

"You're curious?"

"Yes." He turned his head toward me. He laid down his paintbrush, picked up his drink, twirled the ice cubes thoughtfully with his finger.

"So, what are you curious about?"

"I'm curious to know how anyone could be so stoned and still be that lucid." Chuckling, he flicked cold water from the drink onto my face.

Chapter 31

Accusations

My left eye was still raging red from the CS powder. (Earlier, when carefully pouring tear gas powder into an empty mosquito repellent bottle, a tiny, swirling cloud of the fine powder had magically risen straight up and touched my eye. I had managed to set the CS container down and run to the latrine to wash out the burning fireball in my eye.)

The door to my hooch opened and in walked Felds, without knocking.

"You after that hooch maid?" Felds asked with a leer. He nodded toward the homely Vietnamese woman who was polishing my boots. One of the benefits of our unit. They hired women to clean our rooms and polish our boots.

"You kidding?" I said. I thought the question was ridiculous. She was too plain to work in the bars, besides she did a good job with the room and I didn't want to screw it up. "She doesn't appeal to me."

"Some morning you ought to fuck her with a piss hard on. You ever fuck with a piss hard on?" His beady eyes were pin points in the broad jowly face.

"The senior ncos and the officers got all the good looking ones." I said.

"Hell, put a bag over her head." He wouldn't drop it.

"Guess I'm ready to go." I grabbed my rucksack, threw it over one shoulder, and headed toward the chopper pads.

"I've put in for a field commission, I'm going to be an officer," he said proudly as we walked.

"That's nice."

The mission was a local. We were going southeast of the camp about ten kilometers. Part of recon's job was running local recons to check for enemy activity in the vicinity of our camp.

They dropped us into a lush rain forest. A gentle, clear stream ran parallel to our designated course.

Ahead of me in the file, I watched Felds' huge thighs rub together laboriously. His uniform became sweat soaked before anyone else's was even damp.

Without warning, the SCU all spoke rapidly to one another, broke ranks and ran toward a peculiar tree. They dropped their packs, gathered round the tree and started picking fruit.

Felds and I stood with our mouths agape. The tree had a tiny clearing around it. Its limbs were covered with what appeared to be orange slices. Felds sat on a dead tree at the edge of the clearing and wiped sweat from his brow.

Bo ran over to me, handed me several of the fruits, and said, "You eat, number one, vely rare."

I looked at the translucent yellow object in my hand. It was as though one had peeled an orange, then separated the slices. I took a bite of one. It was good, more pithy than an orange, but ripe and sweet and full of juice.

So we had a feast of fresh fruit. The SCU filled their packs with the slices before we moved on. I was nonplused. I'd never seen the SCU so excited and they'd never broken ranks like that for any reason.

Later in the day we heard an explosion in the distance. Moving slowly toward the direction of the blast, we came to a pool of blood with a trail of blood leading away from it. We followed the trail of blood to the stream, where it disappeared. Whoever was hurt walked up the stream to avoid leaving a trail. Beside the steam were khaki fatigues hung on sticks, drying. Further up the steam was a little hooch built across the water. Inside was a supply of rice. The hooch looked relatively comfortable. The floor was woven of native vines.

"Suppose Charlie was rigging up a booby trap and it backfired?" Felds whispered.

I shrugged my shoulders. Empty cans of red mackerel were strewn about. "He's not much of a housekeeper."

―・ ―※+※ ―・

"Sergeant Acre, will you come up to the orderly room?" Felds asked.

"OK," I said, wondering why the formality.

The SGM had finished his tour. We'd gotten a new company first sergeant, an E-8, whom I didn't know well. He was a braggart, on his fifth or sixth tour. He seemed mainly concerned with making sure the younger ncos knew how tough he was.

I stepped inside the orderly room. Felds was in front of the first sergeant's desk. We were in a triangle, the two of us standing, the first sergeant sitting behind his desk.

"What's up Top?" I asked.

Felds face swelled up even bigger, got redder. "Sergeant Acre, I was looking for you last night, so I stepped into your room." He put his hands on his hips, raised his voice. "I smelled pot in your room!"

"Now Sergeant Felds," the first sergeant interrupted. His voice was as big as his forearms. "Are you accusing Sergeant Acre of smoking pot?"

Felds twitched and rubbed his cheek. His voice was shrill. "I smelled pot in his room, I know what pot smells like!"

"Was Sergeant Acre in the room?"

"Well," he hesitated, "no."

"Let me remind you Sergeant Felds, this is a very serious charge you are raising, a very serious charge." The first sergeant looked at me. "Where were you at the time, Sergeant Acre?"

"I suppose I was at the club," I answered.

Felds, his voice still piercing, "I'm not going to the field with a pot smoker. I know pot when I smell it, and I'm not taking any chances!" He poked the air toward me with his finger, the redness in his face spreading to his neck.

"Now, just wait a minute, I want you to be aware of the seriousness of these charges, did you or did you not see Sergeant Acre smoking pot?" the first sergeant looked intently at him.

"No, but it doesn't . . . ."

"All right!" the first sergeant interrupted, slamming his hand on the desk. "I've looked at the records and Sergeant Acre has been running recon since he's been here, and he has a good record, and a good reputation. You're leveling a very serious charge without any direct substantiation . . . ."

"But . . . ."

"You are the ranking nco, if you and Sergeant Acre can't get along, then I'll have to put him on another team. Will that satisfy you?" He looked at Felds again, it was clear that the question was really a statement.

Felds deflated. "All right," he said, after some hesitation.

"Fine, then that should take care of it. Sergeant Acre, you're off team Sickle, I'll find another assignment for you. Felds, I'll let you know who your radio operator will be. That's all." He looked at the door, making it clear that we were to leave.

Felds left first, I was on my way out. "Sergeant Acre, just a minute, I want to talk to you," the first sergeant said.

I turned and walked back toward his desk. He met me in the center of the room. Looking me in the eye he put his huge hand on my shoulder, gripped the muscle between thumb and forefinger and squeezed. The pain shot through my head and shoulder. We stood eye to eye. I tried not to flinch. "I'm telling you this time that those are serious charges." He squeezed the muscle harder. "You keep your nose clean and don't fuck up, do you get my drift?"

We looked into each other's eyes for a long time. I thought I'd faint from the pain, but I didn't move.

"OK, first sergeant, I get your drift."

He released my shoulder. "I want good recon missions and I don't want to be a fucking nurse maid. You guys learn to get along."

"Most of us get along, First Sergeant," I said.

"Don't push it, get out of here!"

I leaned against the wall of the hooch for some time, thinking it over. I'd heard of guys smoking pot in the field, but I didn't know anybody who did, or would even consider it. At least I wasn't going to the field with Felds any more, but I regretted leaving the SCU I felt so close to. The new first sergeant wasn't such a bad sort after all. I watched a fuck-you lizard clinging to the window pane.

He stood very still, waiting for a bug, little suckers on his feet keeping him attached. His throat puffed out and he started talking, in the famous tongue that only a GI in Vietnam could decipher, "Fuhkwew, fuhkwew, fuhkwew."

Chapter 32

Into the Void

The next day I went to the SCU's barracks and told them I was off the team. The radio I'd given them was sitting on the window ledge, playing twangy Vietnamese music. It was the only appliance in the barracks, a large, screened, open room, with dirt floors and wooden bunks.

"Why you off team?" Bo wanted to know.

"Felds doesn't like me cause I smoke pot."

He put his thumb and finger to his lips in a smoking motion. His face was the question. Few of the Vietnamese or Nungs smoked pot, they liked to drink. The inevitable comment was that it made one dinky dau. I didn't know what they'd think, but I'd already decided to tell them the truth.

Bo spoke to the other team members who had gathered around. Immediately they were all protesting at once, complaining in Chinese.

"You no team Sickle, we no go field," Bo said. The rest shook their heads in unison.

It was a thought, but I knew it wouldn't work. Around me stood this remarkable, exotic bunch I felt so close to. Those shrewd, yet transparent, oriental eyes. At least they hadn't judged me so harshly.

In the middle of the night Charlie lugged three rockets close to camp and fired them at us. The whole place was awakened by their terrorizing whistle. Two hit the club, the third left a crater in the road between the TOC and the club. They must have aimed for the TOC and missed. One of the rockets crashed through the club's roof, then careened to the side, tearing a random path through the walls. The other rocket came through a side wall and went out the other side before exploding.

Captain Peasdale, the officer in charge of the club, had finished his tour and left the country the week before. When they checked the books to pay for the repairs, it was discovered that the club was several thousand dollars in the red. A strange situation since the club had been several thousand dollars in the black at the start of Captain Peasdale's tour, and had showed a profit the entire year. Everybody thought that the captain had absconded with the club's money.

All the enlisted men were mad as hell. We'd even had to buy the beer out of our own pockets for the teams coming out of the field.

The officers didn't say anything, it was an embarrassment for them. Their embarrassment was compounded by the fact that they'd just gotten together and built a separate officers club, partly at the urging of the XO, who was concerned about the officers "fraternizing" with the enlisted.

The next night there was a big ruckus. We heard confused shouting and anxious voices, so we stepped outside to see what was going on.

It was a commotion at the officer's club. Crimmings was sitting on one of the platforms of the obstacle course picking his teeth, watching the officers milling around outside their club. Smoke was pouring out the doors and windows.

"What's going on over there?" Rick asked him.

"Somebody threw a smoke grenade in the back door," he answered, lighting a cigarette. In the flickering light of the zippo, his bushy blonde mustache curled up along with a big grin.

"A smoke grenade? Bet that scared the hell out of them," Rick said.

"Yeah, I'll bet it did, could have been a frag just as easy," Crimmings snickered. "When it hit the floor you can bet it sounded just like a frag. They were falling all over each other trying to scramble out of there."

"Any idea who did it?" I asked.

"Nope, somebody with a sick sense of humor, that's for sure," he said.

"Wonder what color smoke it was," Rick said.

"Yellow," Crimmings answered, still smiling.

Sau, the point man on team Sickle, appeared from the darkness. He held something out to me. "Here, you take, number one for you."

I took the article and held it in the light of my cigarette lighter. It was a little smiling Buddha, carved of teak. I was touched. "Thank you Sau, I really appreciate this, I'll always keep it."

"You no team Sickle, you go other team now?" Sau asked.

"Yeah, that's right Sau."

"Felds number ten, you no go field team Sickle, we no go field," he said angrily.

"I can't do anything about it Sau, it's good of you to say that, and I'm glad you feel that way." I knew they'd wind up going to the field anyway. They'd have to unless they wanted to quit, and quitting would mean being instantly drafted into the Vietnamese army. "We'll still be friends."

"Felds go field, number ten, you go field, number one. All team no like Felds," he said.

"Well Sau, maybe Felds will go somewhere else soon," I said.

"You go Chinee team?"

"I don't know yet."

A piece of styrofoam packing from the fridge made a good shelf when it was nailed to the wall. I set the Buddha inside it, on its own little shelf. Rick painted the rest of the white styrofoam with designs and flowers. I thought of Ling and her friends and their altars. The Buddha now had its place in our hooch.

The smoke grenade incident was never mentioned by any of the officers. It was as though nothing had happened. Like Crimmings said, it could have been a fragmentation grenade instead of a smoke grenade.

Felds ran several more missions with team Sickle, then quietly disappeared from CCS. He got his field commission. A field commission meant he would have to be stationed with another unit, it was standard procedure for a man going from enlisted to officer's rank to be transferred. Maybe he deserved it.

The military was a huge machine, a gigantic creature made of flesh and steel, which spread itself out on this tropical rain forest, grabbed a foothold, then ground forward, gears meshing and grinding. When pondering the enormity of this beast, especially when I was in an airplane, I marveled at what a small cog I was inside its innards.

Sometimes the beast seemed powerless to deal with the frustrations that Charlie offered. Viet Cong would sneak in and prick its underbelly and make it bleed; it would raise up its great head and spew fire in fits of undirected rage, burning and destroying everything around it. Then it would settle into a semi-calm, only to be poked by Charlie again, provoked once more to expend its fury.

The NVA was a snake, slithering down the edge of the country, through Laos and Cambodia, quietly pursuing its goal, then striking and burying poison fangs into some vital appendage of the beast.

Our mission was the eye of the beast, as it tried to peer into the den of the snake, to follow its path, to see it shed its skin, to find its fangs, to watch it coil.

Some psyops idiot had come up with the idea that we should scatter leaflets throughout the jungle. The leaflets showed a drawing of the jungle, with eyes peering out. The caption read, "Special Commando Unit. We see you, but you don't see us." They were pissed when we refused to do it. Somebody got a unique bunch of scratch pads, along with good souvenirs to take home and lie about, to help affirm my later theorem, the frequency and amplitude and bravado of the war stories are inversely proportional to the truth of the teller's combat experience.

My inner life was as large as my place in the military machine was small. Much was being taken away, old beliefs and assumptions faded, new ones were hard to define, hard to find.

My concerns had gone from trying to get enough money together to put a new set of tires on my '55 Chevy, studying for my next calculus test, to making sure my weapon operated flawlessly, learning to breathe silently and move quietly while my heart raced, to something vital and primal, staying alive. Yet it was not a continual subject of concern and thought, it was rather a condition, a state of being.

The old life didn't seem real anymore, it didn't seem to have ever been real, or to have ever existed. Yet I dreamed and hungered for cheeseburgers and milkshakes.

In the night as I lay awake, in great, long, impossible reaches of the imagination, I yearned for a place I'd once called home. But I knew that I'd left something behind that I could never return to, I'd stepped over the edge, into a chasm, where death was as real as a '55 Chevy or a calculus test.

When the basic fight or flight response is known, when it floods into consciousness and becomes a primal force, without repression or sublimation, it is a genie out of the bottle; it is a daemon, the daemon that confronts death.

The stars seemed constant. I stood under the starlit sky and watched them. I could touch the sky.

Chapter 33

Away

Bangkok was my choice for R&R. Several of us went at the same time. It was rainy season anyway, a convenient time for us to be gone. First we flew to Saigon. Steve had left recon and had secured a job at the embassy. He met us at Tan Son Nhut airfield and took us to the SOG safehouse somewhere in Saigon. It was an old French estate, with stone walls and wrought iron fences. Vietnamese soldiers guarded the huge, rusty, wrought iron gate.

Inside, he wrote passes to allow us downtown in civilian clothes. Then we went to his rented apartment, somewhere else in the morass that was Saigon. We stayed at his place for two days, while waiting for our plane to Bangkok.

A Saigon taxi was a motorized rickshaw, a motorcycle that looked like a backward tricycle. There was room for two passengers. The driver sat on a motorcycle seat behind handlebars, the passengers were in front on an open bench seat. Riding in one of the things was a thrill and peril unequaled anywhere. The driver tore out under full power, with you in front for a bumper, racing in and out of a river of Honda 50s, Lambrettas, and military vehicles, mostly deuce-and-a-halfs. The driver's motions were totally unexpected and sudden, keeping you in a perpetual state of imbalance on your seat.

On my first excursion to downtown Saigon to see the notorious Thu Do Street, we passed a deuce-and-a-half that was stopped in the middle of the road.

The driver was standing beside his vehicle talking to the MPs while a Vietnamese man railed at them, waving his arms. Inside the radiator of the truck, perversely stuck like a mosquito or grasshopper, was a "cowboy" and his Honda 50.

Cowboy was a term used for young Vietnamese men, purported to be mostly draft dodgers, who dressed wildly in bell bottoms and Beatle boots, and drove around Saigon in a frenzy committing all kinds of petty crimes, from grabbing watches off GI's wrists as they rode by, to selling drugs and other black market activities. The Vietnamese also called them hippies.

Rick and I were taking in the city, walking through a ramshackle area close to downtown, when a Vietnamese woman in her cone hat approached from an alley and said, "You want sucky sucky?"

I turned to Rick, "What do you think, you want sucky sucky?"

He grinned, "Why not, we've got time."

"How much?" I asked.

"Fie hunre pe," she said.

"Hell of a deal," Rick chuckled.

She turned and motioned for us to follow. We followed her, squeezing through a maze of twisting and turning narrow pathways, passing doorway upon doorway, women working at washing, hanging up clothes to dry, sweeping concrete floors. I completely lost my sense of direction.

"Hope we can find our way out of here," I said quietly to Rick.

"This is unreal, must be fifty thousand people living here," he said.

Finally the woman stopped at a door and went inside, again motioning for us to follow. A younger woman, apparently her daughter, gave us our money's worth in turn, in a partitioned side of the room. Then the first woman led us back to the street.

Bill wasn't so lucky. He went through the same routine, but they lifted his wallet at some opportune moment in the deal. They got his money for R&R. "Hey Bill, hear they've got eight hundred dollar blow jobs in Saigon." He heard about it for a long time.

At Steve's apartment we drank and smoked and relaxed. He had a beautiful bar of hand carved teak. He also had a new record, by somebody else we'd never heard of, Santana. We were fascinated by the album cover, which from one perspective appeared as a beautiful woman, from another it was a lion's head.

Steve gave me a thousand dollars in MPC and asked me to bring back greenbacks for him. This was one of the ways to make money. He'd take the greenbacks and sell them on the black market for double the money in MPC, buy a money order with the MPC, and send two thousand home.

Going through customs the guy ahead of me got busted. The customs people ran a wire down his bottle of talcum powder. There was something in the bottom. They emptied out the talc, and at the bottom was a plastic bag with pot in it. They took him to a little room off to the side. Good bye R&R. For two dollars the dummy could have bought enough good Thai pot in Bangkok to last him a month.

— ⊞⊞ —

In Bangkok, after we rented rooms, we went to find women. The taxi driver took me to the bordello. I chose an attractive Thai and spent the night with her. She was about five feet tall, slender, with black hair and eyes. Her name was Warapon. I decided she was OK, so I said, "Let's go to the beach."

She arranged everything. The next morning we got on a bus and headed south. I hardly recognized her. Without the false eyelashes and make-up she was a different person.

We rode the bus to the coast to a paradise called Pattaya.

She had arranged for a room at a small motel. It had eight or ten rooms. It was only paces away from a beautiful coast line. The area was mostly small cottages, apparently owned by foreigners or people in the city, for most of them were unoccupied.

We watched the waves roll in, the water was blue and beautiful, the rhythm was hypnotically soothing.

I pointed to several small islands a mile away. "Lets go out there."

She nodded and disappeared inside the motel. In a few minutes she appeared, accompanied by an old Thai man whose front teeth were missing. She spoke to him in Thai. He nodded, smiling. We followed him to a boat that was moored at a small pier. It was an old fishing boat with an ancient one-lunger engine. He fired the engine up, it spewed black smoke, then blue smoke, then sputtered like an old washing machine motor at two or three hundred rpm.

The seas were calm and the day was clear and hot. He took us to the far side of one of the islands, where we spent the afternoon snorkeling. The boat bobbed lazily beside us in the water. I was charmed by the variety of coral and fish, a multitude of colors and shades and sizes and shapes.

For dinner we went to the restaurant, which was built on a pier over the water. The tables were set with white cloth and china. The waiters were dressed in white tuxedos. The tables were arranged on tiers so that every table had a clear view, facing the piano. A lovely Thai woman dressed in a white sequined gown sang romantic songs, accompanied by a man on the piano. The atmosphere was beguiling, peaceful. The music enchanted while the sound of the ocean soothed.

I was hungry for steak and had a fine filet. We drank wine and had rich, strong coffee after the meal, luxuriating in the ambiance.

While watching the singer I reached toward the ashtray to flick my cigarette. At the same moment the waiter was reaching over my shoulder to pour coffee. The fire of my cigarette buried itself in the soft skin between his thumb and forefinger. I was aghast and apologized profusely. Instead of dropping the steaming pot of coffee in my lap, the waiter calmly finished pouring my coffee before withdrawing the pot, setting it down, and wiping the ash from his hand. Warapon saw the whole episode. I explained how embarrassed I was, and asked her what an appropriate tip would be, then doubled it.

We spent the week in one of three places. At the ocean, at the restaurant, or in bed. It was exactly where I wanted to be, in a strange romantic place near the ocean, with a woman I'd never known, surrounded by people I'd never met.

We lay together at night and tried to communicate. Her English was fair, but not good. She told me about herself. She saved money to go to the United States someday. Her family lived in northern Thailand. Someday if I came back to Bangkok she would take me to northern Thailand.

We became fairly well acquainted in a weeks intimacy, despite the fact that it was her livelihood, and we'd most likely never meet again. It was better acquainted than I'd ever been with any American woman. There was no affectation, nothing to be gained, nothing to be lost, no reason for leverage. Simply, two people sharing time.

I hated to leave her, when R&R was over I didn't bother to exchange my Thai currency back into American. I simply handed her everything that was left, away from the taxi driver or anyone else who might want a percentage.

As the taxi pulled away, taking me back to the airport, she waved goodbye, with probably only a few hours before her work day began again, our eyes fastened together till she was gone. One memory remains, as vivid as today. There were tears in her eyes, and mine.

Chapter 34

A Real Green Beret

In Saigon, it was a cool, cloudy day. Crimmings and I walked up and down Thu Do street, watching the crowd, admiring the women, eyeing the cowboys racing by on Hondas, window shopping. We passed by a couple of young Vietnamese men hanging around the sidewalk. One of them pointed to the Rolex on my wrist.

"You sell watch?" he asked, coming up beside me and reaching for my wrist.

"No," I said, pulling my arm away from his grasp.

"I give you two hundre dollar," he said.

Just what I'd paid for it at the PX.

"No," I said again.

He and his friend stayed beside us.

"I give you three hundre dollar," he offered.

"No," I said, but I was thinking. I'd spent over eight hundred dollars in Bangkok, and was nearly broke.

"I give you three hundre dollar and fie thousan p," he said.

This time I couldn't resist the thought. Two hundred dollars to buy another watch, assuming I could find one again, which was unlikely, a hundred dollars profit, and five thousand piasters to spend in the bar that night. I stopped walking and turned to the man. "You'll give me three hundred dollars," I raised three fingers, "and five thousand piasters?" I raised five fingers on the other hand.

He shook his head rapidly, "Yes, I give you three hundre dollar, an fie thousan p." He smiled broadly. I looked at his clothing. He was dressed in a red sports shirt, slacks and black Beatle boots. The cowboys all wore Beatle boots.

"OK, I'll sell you the watch," I said, finally.

"You come back ten minute, I have money," he said.

"OK, I'll go drink a cup of coffee and come back in ten minutes," I said.

Crimmings and I went to a nearby coffee shop and found a table. "What do you think?" I asked.

"Sounds like a deal to me," he said.

"I wouldn't sell it if I wasn't so broke," I said, "probably won't be able to find another one like it. This is the only one I've seen." I looked at the stainless Rolex GMT on my wrist. The watch I'd wanted for so long before finally finding one at the PX.

"So, don't sell it," he said.

"No, I think I will."

We met them at the same spot. We stepped into an alley between shops, one of the Vietnamese closed the wooden gate. Crimmings watched through the gate for MPs. I eyed the alley for signs of trouble.

"I have money," he said. He reached into his pocket, took out a roll of bills, and counted the money into my open palm. Three hundred dollars MPC, the current issue, and five thousand piasters.

I paused momentarily with the money in my hand and the watch on my wrist, thinking, "I ought to fuck him and take the money and the watch. No, he might have a gun or knife, might be a gun trained on me right now." I took off the watch and handed it to him.

He stuffed it into his pocket, looking over his shoulder nervously, and said, "Maybe MP come, I roll up for you." In one quick motion, he plucked the bills from my hand, rolled them up, put a rubber band over the roll, and stuck it back into my still open hand.

They went one way, and we went the other. I was smiling and singing a happy song. "Boy, what a deal," I said. I pulled the rubber band off the roll and fanned the bills. On the outside of the roll was a single five hundred piaster note, then two one hundred piaster notes, the rest were ten piaster notes. I was in shock.

Crimmings laughed like a hyena. "You've been fucked by a cowboy!"

"Oh, fuck! I can't believe this!" I exclaimed. "What a fantastic sleight of hand trick!"

We went back to the spot where the deal was made, but of course they were long gone. Suddenly the sea of passing oriental faces all looked the same. I was angry and embarrassed.

"Hell with it, I've got enough money here to buy us each a couple of drinks, lets go to the bar."

"Fine with me," Crimmings answered.

We stepped into a bar and I ordered us each a drink. I looked sheepishly at Crimmings' reflection smiling maliciously in the mirror behind the bar.

The place had a juke box. We were in civilian clothes. I was glad. In the middle of our second drink somebody played the "Ballad of the Green Berets." "Silver wings upon their chests, these are men, America's best, one hundred men they'll test today, but only three will win the green beret."

Crimmings cracked up. He slapped me on the back. "Thanks for the drink, old buddy. Three in a hundred, hell, you're one in a million."

"That's a hundred dollar drink, you better enjoy it, you bastard."

Chapter 35

Revelations

Ban Me Thuot had gone through some changes. The Air Force's F model hueys were falling out of the air. Two gunships crashed while I was on R&R, killing an Air Force lt. colonel, a major, and two captains. They crashed shortly after leaving the chopper pads. The investigation simply revealed that the choppers had too many hours, without replacement of critical parts. The F models were grounded until parts could be obtained, and the Army choppers at the 155 compound started supporting us. The 20th Special Operations Squadron, known as the Green Hornets, was the only organization of its kind. They were permanently attached to CCS, and lived on the CCS compound. Thus a special closeness developed between the Green Hornets and Recon.

Another incident was a major shock. My medic friend, Jerry, was dead. He'd died by his own hand, shot in the head by the .38 that he'd kept next to his bed. There was only one round in the revolver. It was a matter of conjecture whether he'd killed himself on purpose, or had lost playing roulette. An nco acquaintance of his said he played roulette a lot. I remembered his comment about a .38 being more fun when I'd asked why he didn't carry a .45.

Rick and I found our favorite seats downtown at the bar. The familiar black vinyl booths with white stuffing poking through the rips and tears, the wobbly tables, it seemed almost like home.

"I still just can't believe it, I knew he was upset, but I just can't believe he did it on purpose," I said, referring to Jerry's death, which was plaguing me.

"Maybe he was playing roulette, there's no way to tell is there?" Rick asked.

"I figure, if he did kill himself, he loaded one shell on purpose, just to confuse everyone," I said, staring at my drink, pondering the little black flecks suspended in the ice cubes. Finally I came back to the present. "Heard anybody say how the support is from the 155 choppers?"

He shrugged his shoulders. "I heard they're doing OK, everybody misses the Green Hornets' gun runs, but other than that guess there's no problem."

"Yeah, those figure eights over your head are hard to beat."

The Air Force ship's miniguns were mounted in the doors, which meant the crew chief and door gunner fired them. On the Army choppers the miniguns were mounted on the skids and the pilot fired them, so they couldn't make the figure eight passes directly over your head, instead they came in runs parallel to your position. We much preferred the Green Hornets' method of support. The crew chief and door gunner could direct very precisely the awesome firepower of their miniguns, bringing it in as close as necessary with pinpoint accuracy. More than one recon team had been saved because of this.

The relative quiet of the sunny afternoon was shattered by a loud Vietnamese voice cursing in English, "God damn fuck Americans! God damn fuck Americans! God damn fuck Americans!"

We looked toward the door to see what the ruckus was about.

"What's his problem?" I asked.

The Vietnamese was waving a magazine in his hand, holding it up in the air, continuing to curse Americans.

Rick looked puzzled. "That's Beaver, the interpreter for team Hammer. What's that magazine?"

When Beaver saw us sitting at the booth, he immediately came over to us. There were tears in his bloodshot eyes. He threw the magazine on the table in front of me. "God damn fuck Americans, see what they do!" he yelled. The magazine was the current issue of *Life Magazine*. It was opened to a ten page spread of the massacre at Mai Lai. Beaver continued, half crying, "Mai Lai my home, my brother, my sisters, two sister, my mother, my father, all kill, all kill! God damn Americans."

The magazine was full of pictures of the lifeless bodies of the people at Mai Lai. I had a momentary vision of my own small home town, with the bodies of the people I'd known all my life laying up and down Main Street. Something felt sick inside me.

"These are people you know?" I asked.

"I know all people there," he said.

"What about VC there?" I asked.

"No VC Mai Lai, never, never! Mai Lai my home, my family, I know all people, these people," he pounded his finger on one of the pictures. He pointed to a dead man sprawled on the ground, "My father!" he cried.

"I'm sorry Beaver," was all I could say.

He grabbed the magazine and carried on in the frenzy of his misery, showing it to everyone, talking to the bartender and the girls. The place was quiet as a church. I looked at Rick across the table. His eyes were solemn, deeper than a statue's after one has been absorbed in it for a long time.

"They think Americans are barbarians," he said quietly.

The silence in the bar persisted in the wake of Beaver's torment, until it was shattered again, this time by gunshots from the bar next door. Everyone raced to the door to see what the commotion was. Several GIs were carrying a wounded GI through the court yard toward a jeep. Drops of blood fell from the heel of his boot, in macabre cadence with the steps of his buddies toting him. He'd been shot in the leg by a Vietnamese in an argument over a woman.

We decided it was time to leave. We left the bar and headed toward our jeep. As Rick started the engine, I saw something in the ditch.

"Hey, look at that!" I exclaimed.

Lying in the ditch was the Vietnamese colonel who'd shot the GI. We jumped out and ran over to him. He'd been shot in the stomach, apparently by a .45. Most of his life had pumped out of him, drenching his fatigues and soaking the earth around and underneath him.

"Christ they just left him there! What do we do with him?" Rick asked, pressing his handkerchief to the bubbling wound.

An E-6 was riding back to post with us. "We can take him across the street to 155, but they'll just let him die," he said.

"What else can we do with him?" Rick asked.

"Guess that's about it, he's pretty close to dying as it is."

We picked up the limp dripping body carefully, laid him in the jeep and took him quickly to the hospital at 155. He died. We never knew for sure if they tried to save him or not. On the ride back to B-50 I studied my hands. They were covered with the blood of the Vietnamese colonel. I was fascinated, horrified; there it was, on my knuckles, dried on my nails, in the creases of my fingers, Vietnamese blood on American hands.

Chapter 36

Night Jump

The first sergeant introduced Rick and me as "old timers" to a new officer at the TOC. It seemed strange. In one sense it was as though I'd been at B-50 for centuries, forever. In another sense, in the same breath, it seemed that I'd barely been there at all. I couldn't pinpoint the transition from FNG to old timer.

A new operation was in the works. The idea was to send several of us to Okinawa for HALO training (High Altitude, Low Opening, sky diving in other words). Then we'd be dropped into sensitive areas during the monsoon rains, at night. It would be impossible to detect the infiltration. Before this got under way, however, they wanted us to jump in from helicopters at night. These would be static line jumps from eight hundred feet, just enough time for your chute to open, orient yourself, and hit the ground.

Babysan was to be the team leader for the night parachute infiltration, I was to be the radio operator. It would be a four man operation, two Americans, and two Chinese Nungs.

First we flew to a base near Saigon, where we practiced jumping from helicopters. We jumped nine times, four times in the day, five times at night, with full combat gear. We carried a night vision device, which included an infrared light, and an infrared scope. We could flash these lights to each other, and see one another's light in the dark. This was to enable us to link up in the darkness.

We rehearsed a strict procedure. A captain from the TOC was in charge of the operation. As the chopper approached the drop zone, he gave us the notification, "two minutes," then "one minute," then "get ready," then "go!"

Jumping from a chopper was fun. You sat in the door, looking out ahead toward the approaching drop zone. When the command "get ready" was given, you stood on the skid, then just stepped off into thin air at the command of "go!" The count down was an extra shot of adrenaline at each command, as the anticipation built toward the approach of the jump.

We came back to Ban Me Thuot to be deployed to the launch site. During the couple of days we waited, I started getting worried. I thought about the letter from my mother so many months ago, the one about the rumor of my being MIA during a parachute jump. At the time I'd written home that it was ridiculous, we weren't even jumping. Now I was going to jump. I thought about Jim's prescience about dying. I wondered if through some strange twist of the ethers, they'd known back in the World, before I did, that I was MIA.

I decided I wasn't going. I tried to step in a hole and sprain my ankle. My ankles were too strong. Weak ankles all my life, now I couldn't even sprain one on purpose.

I talked to Hensley about my reservations. I didn't tell him about the letter from home. He said he'd go for me. He wanted to jump in. I thought about the chopper crew chief's premonition, his regret at letting someone go in his place. I decided no one was going in my place.

The 155 choppers would be our support. The Air Force F models were still grounded.

I tried to rationalize. Babysan was the best, the very best. No one had ever been killed on a mission with him.

The day of the operation we overflew the drop zone. The chopper flew over a mountain, the only landmark in the area, and headed toward the drop zone at an azimuth of 270 degrees, or due west. It was an area with very high trees and hardly any undergrowth. It was easy to understand why there was no undergrowth. We could see Charlie down there in Khakis, burning off the area, controlling the fires. Fires were everywhere.

I pointed to the figures below, shoveling dirt, digging firebreaks. The captain looked at them and nodded his head. "They won't be working at night," he yelled over the sound of the chopper.

"Great," I thought.

Back at the launch site I checked and rechecked my gear. My rucksack was attached to the parachute web gear, in front, beneath my reserve chute. My weapon was attached to the front of the ruck, immediately under the reserve, where I could reach it first.

Night came, the full moon rose, one in the morning came, two in the morning. Then we were in the air on the chopper, sitting in the door.

When the mountain appeared in the moonlit haze, the chopper made an abrupt turn toward the west directly over it. I leaned out, looking in the direction we were traveling. The ground below was mysterious looking, hazy silhouettes of tall trees, red coals here and there from burned out fires. I tried to peer into the darkness to see the approach of the drop zone.

Suddenly the captain hit me on the back, yelling "Go!"

"What?" I screamed. No two minute warning! No one minute warning! No get ready! Just "Go?"

"Go!" he yelled again.

I looked to the other side of the chopper. Babysan was gone. The Chinese was still there. I looked out the back of the chopper. Babysan was floating out there behind us. I jumped. While I was falling, before my static line pulled out the chute, I fastened on the full moon. I asked for help to get to Babysan. I knew I had to get to him, at least within range of our lights. A team split was a disaster. Something bigger than myself reached out to me, something bigger than the full moon.

The chute opened. I turned to face Babysan, so I'd drift in his direction. I was totally concentrated on moving toward him, jumping at 800 feet left little time. I felt something pulse through my being, like a magnet impelling me toward him.

Then I was above the trees. We'd missed the drop zone. There was a fire directly below the tree I was falling into. I hoped it wasn't a camp fire. I hit the tree, crashing head over heels through the limbs and leaves. At the first limb, time changed, and went into slow motion. It felt like hours falling through the tree. My body hit a limb, I spun down head first, my head bounced off a limb, then my elbow, I was turning over and over, falling, falling, so slowly, as though in water. The pain of each impact was slow and agonizing, yet distant, unreal.

After what seemed several hours, I hit the ground with a thud, entangled in the parachute shrouds. Time snapped to normal. Bang! An AK was fired. I pulled out my knife and cut myself loose. If Charlie had been at the bottom of the tree, he'd have nailed me. He was there, and close, the AK hadn't been far away. I got my weapon loose, pulled on my ruck, peered through the night vision device. Flash!

Babysan was fifteen feet away! I couldn't believe my good fortune. I flashed my light to him and crept in his direction.

He'd landed in a tree too, and was also not injured. The two Chinese were nowhere in sight. I got on the radio, established contact, gave the code for team split. The FAC radioed back that he was flying with his lights off because he was taking fire from the ground.

"What now?" I whispered to Babysan.

"Find the SCU," he whispered. "Charlie's got us spotted, somebody saw us come down, that's why they fired the single shot. They don't know exactly where we are though or we'd already be in deep shit."

"This isn't deep shit?" I thought. "We're going to go stumbling around in the dark looking for two Chinese dressed like NVA, in the middle of a bunch of other NVA? Fuck!" The two Chinese didn't have any infrared devices. We'd wanted some for them, but the people at the TOC didn't want to trust the Chinese with them.

Our whispered communication was interrupted by the sound of automatic AK fire. "They're taking shots at the FAC again," Babysan whispered.

We started carefully working our way through the area in ever widening circles. Even though the moon was full, under the trees we could barely see any outlines. Babysan stopped and crouched. I did the same. He pointed. Ahead of us three figures were moving stealthily. We sat quietly, until they passed.

"This is a fucking mess," Babysan whispered.

I shook my head in the darkness. We continued to walk in bigger circles, with no luck. No sign of either of the Chinese. The FAC pilot asked what we wanted to do. We said we'd wait and keep trying to find the other two men.

We sat for an hour, peering into the darkness. A shadow-like figure appeared in front of me. I watched it walk slowly toward me, just a dim outline. Then I could see that he had an AK. I had my weapon pointed at him, my finger on the trigger. He continued to come toward me, until he was a foot away, then he knelt down and put his face directly in front of mine, so that our noses were nearly touching. It was our interpreter. "Where in the hell have you been?" I whispered.

"VC," he whispered, pointing his finger in a circle, "I fall, hit head."

He led us to the place where he'd landed. His parachute had caught in a tall tree, leaving him hanging high in the air. He'd rappelled down, but he was too high. His rappelling rope was too short, fifteen feet off the ground. He'd run out of rope and come crashing to the ground, knocked unconscious. He hadn't seen the other Chinese either.

We waited till dawn. A slick came in and picked us up shortly after dawn, then we circled the area. The Nung on the ground did have an emergency radio; the interpreter got on an emergency radio on the chopper and tried to get in contact with him. He told him to drop a smoke so we could come in and get him. Nothing. We circled for a half hour, when the crew chief said we'd have to go back for fuel soon. We told him to put us back in first before they left.

The copilot spotted red smoke on the ground. The interpreter got on the radio and asked him to confirm that he'd dropped smoke. This time he got an answer.

The chopper got as close as it could to the smoke and set down. We jumped off and ran toward it. About a hundred meters from the chopper we found him, lying on the ground. I grabbed his pack and handed it to the captain, who'd jumped off with us, and was looking lost. The Nung couldn't walk. Babysan and I picked him up and he put an arm around each of our shoulders. He grimaced with pain. We carried him back to the chopper, his legs dragging behind him.

We laid him on the chopper floor, hopped on and were gone.

Both his legs were broken. He hadn't talked on the radio or thrown smoke because Charlie was close. He'd waited until he couldn't hear them, then had taken a chance and dropped the smoke.

Back at Ban Me Thuot everybody was relieved. The whole camp had been awake when they'd gotten the team split message.

The next day the first sergeant came over to our room and asked me about the mission. He said the captain was over there at the TOC telling them that the reason the mission failed was because I hesitated in the door. He said if it wasn't true I should go over there and straighten it out.

I was furious. In the debriefing Babysan and I had just left it alone and not mentioned anything about the way we were jumped. Now the captain was trying to stick it to me. I made it to the TOC in record time, ran down the stairs to the operations room, where the captain was sitting at a desk with the XO.

"Sergeant Acre, we were just talking about you," the XO said.

"Oh really, what were you talking about sir?" I said, bottling my anger.

"Why did you hesitate in the door?" he asked.

"Who says I hesitated in the door sir?"

"The captain here says that's why the mission went wrong."

I was so angry I could have grabbed the captain and choked him, but I managed to keep my cool. "Well sir, the fact of the matter is, I was sitting in the door watching for the DZ, waiting for the two minute warning. You know, two minutes, then one minute, then get ready, then go. That's the way we practiced it, right sir?" I looked at the captain.

His face was getting red as he nodded affirmatively.

"Well sir, all of a sudden the captain hits me on the back and says 'Go' out of nowhere. I asked him what he'd said, he says 'Go' again, so I look out the door of the chopper and there's Babysan floating out there all alone. When I saw him out there floating all by himself, of course I jumped then, I had no choice, now did I?"

The XO looked stone faced at the captain, who was turning unmistakably crimson.

I continued talking. "Of course when I jumped with the radio, the SCU jumped too. And something else sir, believe it or not, Babysan and I landed about fifteen feet apart, we linked up right away, and started looking for the SCU, which was kind of hard, since Charlie was in there looking around too. So if you want to say I hesitated in the door, strictly speaking, I guess that's true, of course I hesitated, when I got a 'Go' out of nowhere, but I landed right beside Babysan. What if he had said something else and I had just jumped out of the chopper in the middle of nowhere by myself? Besides, nobody hit the drop zone. We were all in the trees. Where were we from the drop zone anyway?"

"Is that what happened?" the XO asked the captain.

The captain, noticeably fidgety, said, "Well, more or less."

"OK sergeant, that's all," he said, not taking his eyes off the captain.

Chapter 37

A Matter of Degree

I slipped the magazine into the CAR-15, noted the positive click that indicated it was held firmly in position, ejected it, slid it back in, then drove cartridges into the chamber, ejecting each one onto the cot.

"You know what I think?"

"What do you think?" Rick said.

He was wrapping green tape around the end of his magazine.

We'd been issued the new thirty round magazine for our weapons, one for each American in recon. We were to test it and see how it worked. It was nice to have thirty rounds to carry locked and loaded in the weapon for initial contact.

"I wonder if somebody had a case of the ass for Babysan, so he just 'accidentally' got jumped early out there all by himself. You know how he is, a lot of the officers at the TOC don't like him. Toss me that roll of tape."

I followed suit with my magazine, taping the end. We were taping it because the first team to field test the new thirty round magazine had found it to be excellent, except for one small defect. When sneaking through the jungle with it in their weapons, the bottom unexpectedly fell out, dropping the spring and all the cartridges out onto the ground.

Thoughtfully, Rick rotated the magazine in his hands.

"I don't know, it's something to think about. Does seem strange, the way the whole thing happened."

"Yeah, what if I hadn't been able to land beside him. God, I shudder at the thought. We'd have all been separated. Who knows what would have happened."

"That ought to hold it," he held up the magazine, slid it into his weapon. "Can you imagine having all your bullets fall out on the ground?"

"Talk about a nightmare come true."

He held up his hand, "Hold it Charlie, King's X, I gotta pick up my bullets."

"See you in a few days," I said, grabbing my ruck and heading out the door.

This time it was a local, and it was a platoon sized unit. The word was that the people at the TOC wanted to show more activity around our base camp. I was assigned to carry the radio.

The first day was uneventful, we tromped through the jungle like any other unit larger than a recon team, making all the noise and leaving a trail of broken underbrush typical of such a troop movement. I hated the idea of getting into enemy contact in such a situation. I felt more vulnerable with large numbers of troops.

The second night, we set up camp, even had the luxury of a tent in the inner perimeter, something I'd never done before. At about ten o'clock at night, I suddenly felt a stab of pain in my lower back. It was intense and continuous. We had a medic along with us and I told him about the pain. I could barely talk. He asked me to describe it and felt the area in my back. He told me to lie down in the tent. I lay there all night without sleep, asked for pain killers but he wouldn't give me any because he didn't know what the problem was. By morning the pain still hadn't abated, so they called for a medevac to take me out. The chopper made it at noon.

They took me to the 155 compound, across from the bar where we liked to hang out. One of the doctors x-rayed me, and checked my prostate. I told him the pain wasn't in my ass, it was in my back. When he returned with the x-rays he showed me the problem. I had a small kidney stone lodged in the urethra between my right kidney and bladder. He gave me a shot of Demerol. It wasted me, put me in a semi-unconscious state; the universe became a blur with a distinct center located in my lower back.

I drifted through a fog to another medevac chopper. The chopper took off in a liquid state, flowing through something like water. On the way to Pleiku the medevac landed. The sound of gunfire penetrated the haze in my brain. A Vietnamese soldier was brought in with me and laid on the floor. I could hear voices echoing somewhere. The chopper took off. The Vietnamese started wheezing and gurgling up blood. It ran down the side of his face, onto the steel plate floor, making islands of the little pyramid shaped treads in the steel. In my drugged state the sight of impending death was strangely fascinating. The medic worked quickly over the man, trying to keep him alive. Then he died. I was very close, but far away.

At Pleiku they had two stretchers waiting beside the chopper pad.

"I can walk, I don't need that," I said. I lurched out the door and staggered inside.

I was put in a bay with the wounded. The nurse, the white American nurse, the white, round eyed, full breasted, pretty blonde nurse showed me where to bunk.

"Do you want morphine?" she asked.

"No."

"Kidney stones can be pretty rough, let me know if you change your mind."

"OK."

I lay in the bed, walked around, watched the suffering around me for a week. A Montagnard across from me had no lower jaw. It was just gone. His upper teeth and lip gaped grotesquely.

A Special Forces SFC was at the end of my isle. He had three tubes running out of his chest. What an attitude he had. He laughed and joked and kidded the nurses. Him with a bullet to the chest, through a lung.

My pain was complete, constantly demanding attention. I awoke from sleep at night every few minutes, the knife-like stab dominating even my sleep, ever present. Yet I wanted no pain killer, my pain seemed insignificant compared to the other suffering in the room.

One night early in the morning my fitful dozing was interrupted by the screaming of the Yard directly behind me. The nurse came running to his bed. She plunged her hand deep into his leg beyond the wrist, pinching off a bleeding artery. He'd awakened bleeding to death. She called for more help. A doctor and other nurses came and tied off the artery again.

The nurse brought a box of books from the States, a care package somebody had sent. I was amazed at my state. So dominated by pain, yet so consumed with desire for her. I imagined what her breasts would look like if only I could unzip her white dress. When she left my eyes followed the sway of her hips, savored the curve of her calves.

The box of books was a nice gesture from somebody back in the World. I went through it, looking for something that seemed interesting. All the light reading seemed superficial, it wouldn't come to life. *Crime and Punishment* was the only one that caught my eye, the Russian classic by Dostoevsky. I tried to read it, but couldn't finish it, wondering why they included it in a care package to Nam, it seemed superfluous.

On the tenth day about noon I took my periodic piss in a tin cup. This time I enjoyed the faint clink of something solid landing in the cup, accompanied by a great wave of pleasure, or rather the sudden absence of pain. The stone was out of my system and in the cup. They took it away to be analyzed, told me to drink more water and try to not get dehydrated, and let me go back to Ban Me Thuot.

Back at camp they were surprised to see me. They'd heard mistakenly that I was headed to Tokyo or back to the States.

Fast Eddie asked me about my stay at the 155 compound. "That doctor there is a little strange, I suppose he gave you a finger wave?"

"He said he was checking my prostate," I said. "I told him the pain was in my back not in my ass."

"Yeah, well, he's been checking everybody's prostate, even if they've got a toothache, everybody I've talked to that's gone over there has gotten a finger wave, he's a fucking weirdo," Fast Eddie said, shaking his head and rolling his eyes.

Chapter 38

Boilermakers

The SCU insisted that I come to their party. Every month or so they had a feast, a celebration that they said was a party for Buddha. They asked me to pick up a case of beer and some whiskey for them at the PX.

I stepped into their barracks with the case of beer over my shoulder and four quarts of whiskey in a sack under my arm. They greeted me in unison, welcoming me, pointing to the table that was already set. They'd waited for me.

Each bottle of whiskey I removed from the sack and set on the table was greeted by a louder and more enthusiastic "Number One!"

Song held out a mixture of MPC and Piasters to pay for the booze.

"No sweat, number one chop chop," I said, pointing to the food, indicating that they should keep their money.

It was like a picnic table, with benches along both sides. They'd put three of them end to end, it stretched nearly the length of the barracks. Large, dented, metal bowls sat evenly spaced down the length of the table. Each bowl contained one of three foods. In several of the bowls was boiled chicken, which had been cut into squares, bones and all, with no semblance to the pieces to which Americans are accustomed. The second food was a leafy vegetable that reminded me of the collard greens my grandmother liked so well. The third food was rice.

They directed me to sit. A small bowl of the same metal as the large bowls was put in front of me, along with two chopsticks. One of the SCU opened beers and passed them around the table, while another poured whiskey and coke into glasses.

I ate in the same fashion as they. One filled his small bowl with rice, reached for the bowl of greens or chicken and dropped several pieces onto the rice. The bowl was brought underneath the mouth, and held directly under the chin while one scooped the food into the mouth with the chopsticks. Of course the SCU were adroit with the chopsticks, and by this time I'd at least learned how to use them, but I wasn't good at it. Since I'd heard the process of making nook nam, their version of soy sauce, I declined it. Nook nam was made by filling a gunny sack with fish, and hanging the sack in the sun. A pan was placed under the sack. The liquid that dripped into the pan was nook nam.

When I finished a beer, another was in front of me immediately, the same with the whiskey and coke. When I finished my bowl of rice, they insisted that I take more. After several bowls of rice, I finally shook my head and said, "No, thank you, I really can't eat another bite."

By this time the place was getting loud and rowdy. Bo, who was sitting beside me, nudged me and said, "You take bowl rice, then no eat."

"What are you talking about Bo, I can't eat another bite."

"I know, I know, you see Chinee custom say, if guest not leave food, then he still hungry. Take food, no eat, evlybody know you have enough to eat."

I did as he said, laughing at myself. "You see Bo, in my country, it's considered bad manners to not eat all the food you take."

He nodded his head, smiling. When I left the food in the bowl, the SCU quit pestering me to take more.

Then the coke was being left out of the whiskey, it was straight whiskey chased by beer. One of the SCU would take the floor and make a boisterous toast, the rest of the Chinese would cheer, and they'd all down another shot of whiskey and chase it with beer. If my shot wasn't gone after the toast, they jeered and shook their heads and waited till I drank my shot before another round was poured. I got very drunk, the most I'd been since coming to Nam.

Just before dark the party was interrupted by explosions on the other side of the compound, then by the sound of the siren. We were taking incoming! This struck me as extremely funny. Suddenly I was alone at the table, the SCU were all scrambling to get their flak jackets and weapons or running back to their own barracks.

"Well fuck," I said, reaching for the whiskey bottle sitting in the middle of the table. After a couple of swigs I wobbled toward my own hooch. People were running everywhere, in all directions, shouting instructions, heading for the berm.

I stumbled into my hooch, found my flak jacket, pulled on my ammo belt, picked up my weapon and headed for the formation. Everybody was already there in front of Recon Headquarters, they all had their backs to me, I was the last one to report. That struck me as very funny also. I pointed the CAR-15 toward an open area in the compound, flicked off the safety, and ripped off ten rounds on full automatic. Then it was really funny. The whole formation was scrambling to the ground, over sandbag walls, behind buildings, and every one of their weapons was pointed directly at me.

"Ha, ha, ha, you should have seen you guys jump," a voice said from my mouth.

They were getting to their feet, yelling at me and cursing. I laughed louder.

The captain came over to where I stood, took my arm and led me back to my hooch. "You just stay here," he said.

"Right sir." I sat on the ground in front of the hooch, with my weapon across my lap, and descended into drunken unconsciousness.

The night was full of apparitions and dreams. People running by, weapons being fired, choppers taking off, miniguns and rockets, the .50 calibers fired from the berm.

I spent the night in undisturbed pickled sleep.

Chapter 39

To Stay or Not to Stay

The sunlight was hot on my face. Squinting, I peered through the red blaze that was my eyelids. My body ached and my head felt encased in lead. The CAR-15 was still lying across my lap. Between the hooches a green blob was on top of the picnic table. It was Hensley curled up in a poncho liner. He'd taken to sleeping on the picnic table lately.

I stood up stiffly, stretching my aching limbs, and stepped inside the hooch.

"Hey, what happened to you," Deak asked.

"Not so loud, my head is splitting," I said.

"Turned into a regular juicer have you?" Rick said.

"Oh, the SCU and their party for Buddha," I moaned. "What happened last night?"

"We got a few mortar rounds, they sent the choppers up, even thought Charlie was probing the perimeter once," Deak said.

"How long you guys been up?"

"Since seven, we tried to wake you up a couple of times, but we finally decided to let you be," Rick said. "How can anybody sleep through a fucking war?"

"I don't know what it was, but it wasn't sleep," I shook my head, "it was chasing the whiskey with beer that did it."

"Oh shit."

"Yeah, the SCU were really soaking it up."

"What the hell was the deal with ripping off the rounds? Do you remember that?"

"I remember it."

"Not a very funny joke."

"No, not very funny, you should have seen you guys though."

"You could have gotten yourself shot."

"Yeah."

I wandered around the compound, thinking about the night before. That was a crazy thing to do. I could have easily gotten myself killed. Why had it seemed so funny? Why did it still seem so funny? Maybe I shouldn't extend. Most of the others were already talking about extending for six months, for the free month leave anywhere in the world, and for the early out.

Seeing the dispensary made me think of Jerry, my medic friend. He'd advised me to try for Panama if I didn't want to stay in the Nam. The dispensary seemed a blank spot, a shadow of some past time. As I walked by I could still see him leaning against the wall in the shade, with his arms folded, his balding head and his wry smile. I'd stop and visit a few minutes, he'd tell me some story about the times when the war was young. The empty spot was desolate.

I had orders for Ft. Devins. I didn't want to go back to the States for any kind of garrison duty. It might be OK in some ways, to be in Massachusetts, close to Washington D.C., I could go see the Smithsonian and the Monuments, the Capitol. But something else said no, no way could I see going back to the States with all the spit shining and polishing and bull shit. Besides, Central America was supposed to be the next hot spot. Steve had told me that Central America would be the next place we'd be needed. We'd gotten Che, but that wasn't the end of it, only the beginning.

My head felt a little better after walking around the compound awhile. The SCU razzed me when I passed their barracks. Laughing like crows, they twirled their fingers around their ears, and holding imaginary weapons made mock bursts of automatic weapons fire.

Smiling sheepishly I swatted the air toward them with my hand and hurried on by.

"Hey, Acre, La Dei, La Dei," Tai, the interpreter, was beckoning for me to come over to the barracks. He waved his hand in the curious palm down fashion of the Vietnamese, instead of palm up, as we would do.

"What do you want?" I asked from a distance, expecting more foolishness.

"La Dei, La Dei," Bo and Song joined the interpreter.

Reluctantly, I trudged over to their barracks. They motioned for me to follow them inside.

"Here, for you," Bo said. He held out a picture.

It was a wallet sized picture of him, dressed in camouflaged jungle fatigues, holding a CAR-15, standing in front of a photographer's cardboard set of a cottage surrounded by flowers and shrubs. I was touched, trying not to show my bewilderment at the paradoxical nature of the photo. The set was fantasy-like, Alice in Wonderland stuff. Then the others pressed around, handing me a photo of each of them, obviously taken at the same place.

"For you, you number one, you go United State, you have picture."

"Thank you," I mumbled, trying to suppress the emotions that were erupting. "Bo, where did you guys get these photos taken?"

"Da Lat, number one, yes?"

"Yes, definitely number one," I nodded. "Just one thing I'm curious about though, where did you get the CAR-15 for these pictures?"

He just shrugged his shoulders and smiled, saying something in Vietnamese, then "No problem."

⊶⊷⊷⊶

"What are you doing Rick?" He was leaning on his elbow at the makeshift desk, writing on some military forms.

"Filling out my extension papers," he said, without raising his head.

"You've decided to do it huh?"

"Yeah, I'll run recon awhile longer, then Steve said he can get me a job at the Embassy." He looked up from the papers. "What about you?"

"I don't know, I haven't decided yet."

"We could spent a month in Africa, or Sydney or Hawaii or wherever we wanted," he said enthusiastically.

"That would be fantastic!" I exclaimed, meaning it.

"Steve said he could get us both jobs in Saigon," he twirled his gold peace sign between thumb and forefinger.

"Yeah, wouldn't that be great, we could get an apartment downtown, have our own vehicle." I squeezed the stainless bracelet on my wrist. It was made of rear rotor drive chain from a huey. "Ever think we're tempting fate by staying?"

He hesitated a long moment. "We're just getting good at running recon, besides, if it's your time it's your time, it doesn't matter where you are, you could get run over on the street back in the World."

"That's right," I said. This attitude was prevalent, I doubted whether it was real consolation for him, and I knew it wasn't for me.

I liked the SCU so much, and my American friends were friends like I'd never had before and knew I'd never have again. I felt a strong bond with them. I came to believe fate had somehow brought us all together in this spot in a remote corner of the world for greater purposes that none of us understood. Perhaps I had to believe this, but it was something I believed I sensed first, then thought and felt. Politics and causes were meaningless in this sense. The revolution in the World, and politics and the protests we were hearing about had meaning in their realms, and they were powerful enough to deal with. This fate, this situation, this condition transcended all that, had a deeper meaning to me, and it was very compelling. I didn't want to leave them, it, the realm.

What I didn't tell him was, I was getting the "feeling." The feeling that I was going to die if I stayed. I didn't tell anyone about it. It was getting stronger.

These two forces were in opposition within me, one said stay, the other said leave. As the days passed and the time for a decision came closer, the strife intensified and ravaged me. I found no humor in the irony of this conflict. To go one way was to lose something deeper and more meaningful and more intense than anything I could have ever possibly imagined before. To go the other way could cost me my life. They were special forces.

Chapter 40

Parties and Losses

The bright light team never found Babysan. Some said he was last seen kneeling behind a log, holding his rifle in a firing position, shot many times.

The chopper that should have borne his body set down momentarily at the edge of the chopper pad beside recon company. The chopper's crew chief gently set somebody's web gear, rucksack, and rifle at the edge of the metal grating. While the dust was settling from the departed chopper, we slowly wandered over to the pads. The CAR-15 was leaning against the rucksack. The web gear lay beside the ruck. The canteens were empty, bullet holes had let the water out. The web belt and magazine pouches were stained dark red. The hand grip of the rifle was shattered.

No words were spoken, I guess we were paying tribute around the only remains we would ever see. After a few minutes Top quietly picked the things up and slowly headed in the direction of Supply. He was a powerful man, but his back was bowed under the weight. Twenty-five years in the Army. I wondered how many times he'd had to do this.

They hadn't found the Grit. He was still out there somewhere, alive or dead nobody knew. He'd be officially MIA, even though they had the rest of the bodies.

Four days later, a FAC plane flying over the area detected a pen flare. It was the Grit. He'd gotten a shrapnel wound to the head and had lain out there immobilized. We didn't see him again either. He was sent to Tokyo in critical condition. They made him a new skull out of stainless steel.

Over seventy missions Babysan had. The odds finally went against him.

It was close to Christmas. I was in my hooch getting my gear together. Watson came to the door holding a big fruitcake. The Grit had been his roommate.

"You want a piece of fruitcake?" he offered.

"Sure," I said. He cut a huge wedge and held the tin in front of me. "Man, that's half the darn thing, save some for yourself," I said.

"Don't worry about it," he said. "Come over to my room, I want to show you something." I followed him to his room, where he opened his wall locker. "See this."

"Well, I'll be damned," I said. Fruitcakes were stacked to the top of the locker.

"Every relative I have sent me a fruitcake," he chuckled, smiling with teeth, since he'd recently gotten his partials. "Now eat your fruitcake."

I did, with relish.

Christmas was filled with nostalgia. Everyone seemed lost in his own world, writing home, reading letters from home. Christmas in the Army was always a lonesome time, Christmas in the Nam was especially poignant.

New Years was a different story. It was a twenty-four hour celebration. We packed the club for hours, drinking and raising hell. We had an Australian rock and roll band, and round eyed dancers. Martha Raye came to visit our unit. She roamed around talking with us, giving words of encouragement. Some of the very few words of encouragement I ever had from an American civilian while I was in uniform. She even hugged me and kissed my cheek. I didn't even know who Martha Raye was, except she was somebody famous, and it felt good.

After she left, the party got pretty rowdy. The dancers got raunchy and the band got outrageous. The dancers were dressed in scanty costumes, up on a makeshift half circle stage, around which we drunken soldiers sat lustfully. When they started dancing up close, guys started grabbing them by the ass and rubbing their faces in their crotches.

The chaplain couldn't take any more. He stopped the party and gave us a speech about the way professional soldiers conduct themselves.

Monroe and I got the colonel's cow. Monroe hopped on her back and I led her down the road. The camp was lit by flares and machine gun tracers. Trudging down the red dirt road was the old cud chewing cow with the peace sign on her side, led by one drunken soldier, ridden by another, her peace sign blinking rapidly off and on in the stroboscopic light.

The colonel stopped beside us in his jeep, one alcoholic haze speaking to another alcoholic haze. "Where you guys going with my cow?"

"We're ridin her to the club, sir!" Monroe answered.

"Well, let her go."

"All right sir."

We let her go. She walked over to a patch of grass beside one of the hooches and found an appealing morsel.

Back in the club there was an argument about whether a pen flare was an effective weapon. Guys generally carried one downtown with them, since they looked much like a pen, or small flashlight.

Several guys went outside and found one of the goats. The pen flare was aimed at the goat from a distance of ten feet. The little rocket sped from the flare in a red streak, striking the goat in the side, then spitting red flames from the wound. The goat dropped dead with hardly a complaint.

I walked out to the berm alone and watched the fireworks. All the camps in the distance were ripping off rounds in New Year's celebration. Rounds were erupting from them in all directions, even straight up, like huge Roman candles.

Everybody was acting a little crazy, even for New Years. The Grit was our friend, all fucked up and in the hospital. Babysan was the best of the best, and he was dead.

Chapter 41

Short

January came and I still couldn't make up my mind whether to extend. Everybody who was short talked about it and made a big thing about counting down the days until he left country, especially if he was getting out of the Army when he left the Nam.

"You going to the field again?"

"Fuck no! I'm gettin short."

"The XO is trying to get Recon to stand inspections."

"Fuck him, I'm short."

"What are you doing getting loaded first thing in the morning?"

"I'm short man, fuck it."

I still had two months. I was short, but not short. When I wasn't in the field, I wanted to go in again. The urge for the mystery, the danger, the adrenaline. When I was in the field I didn't want to be there anymore, I was afraid of dying.

I knew there could never be anything like the feeling of topping the crest of a small mountain somewhere in Cambodia, peering through the foliage at a panorama of mountains and forest and clouds that showed no sign of civilization for as far as the eye could see. To know that I was standing in a spot where no other white man had ever stood, quite possibly no man at all had ever stood in some of those places. At these times I envied only one group of men in the entire world, and that was at night, when the moon was full. I'd watch the moon and contemplate the fact that the astronauts had stood on that moon. How intensely I felt, standing in that dense tropical rain forest, one of a very few who'd been there in such circumstances. How those astronauts must have felt! I thought I could imagine!

There was one fear that ate away. I'd awake from a doze during the night just in time to see an NVA soldier standing over me, with his AK pointed at my chest, see the first couple of rounds blaze from the barrel. My sleep was lighter than a cat's.

On one mission with Fast Eddie we were being tracked. We knew about Charlie's method of harassing recon teams. It was a Chinese method. They'd work in three man teams, following a recon team, keeping you spotted, making just enough noise to keep you even more on edge than you already were. They'd wait for a mistake, a chance to set up an ambush and run you into it.

We'd been moving along very slowly, the sweat bees buzzing around our ears, making it difficult to hear anything. We thought we heard something off to our right, so on a hand signal by the team leader we'd all freeze solid. Every time there was a telltale crack of a twig or a rustle of grass off to the side, as Charlie froze too, but just an instant after we did. Everybody on the team was getting skittish, including the SCU, which was exactly Charlie's intention.

We were moving on a carpet of leaves through a beautiful stand of hardwood trees that followed a stream. It was like a boulevard, the trees were lined in natural rows that could have been planted. We played this stop and go, cat and mouse game for hours.

We explored some trenches that circled a hill across the stream. Instead of built up bunkers there were holes dug back into the hill from inside the trenches. The place was deserted, but there were signs of recent habitation, and it was eerie.

We moved on, paralleling the stream and the boulevard of trees. The wind was gentle and whispering, the day was warm but not unbearably hot. The bushes crackled occasionally a few meters away. I wondered if Disneyland had anything like this. I wondered if I'd ever get to see Disneyland. "Where did that come from," I mused, "This is Fantasyland, Disneyland is the World's Fantasyland, this is real, it isn't. No, this is unreal, no this is real." These weren't thoughts, for I wasn't distracted, these were organic events occurring somewhere in the depths of my psyche.

Then an AK's thumping on automatic chopped the stillness into scattered fragments. A millisecond later, the team's weapons returning fire dashed the fragments into splinters.

The fire hesitated and we started leapfrogging away from the direction of the AK. Then it started again, we laid down a base of fire again, the firing quit again.

When the gunbirds were flying figure eights over our heads we were huddled behind a huge downed tree. Rounds were flying everywhere.

I was on the radio, getting the gunbirds coordinated. A new American was on his first mission with us. He wrenched a grenade from his belt, pulled the pin, and threw it in the direction of the enemy. Two seconds, three, four, five, nothing. The grenade was a dud.

"Did you get the pin pulled on that thing?" I yelled over the noise.

He gave me a dirty look, crawled close to the dead tree, poked his CAR-15 over the top and pulled the trigger. Nothing. The weapon jammed. He glanced back at me in disbelief while he stripped the bolt from the weapon. I shook my head, kept talking on the radio.

Fast Eddie was sitting directly across from me. He was scanning the forest with eyes like telescopes. He looked over my shoulder, his eyes zooming in on something behind me, while he whispered, "Duck!"

I ducked, and he fired a burst just inches above my head.

"Not gonna sneak up on my radio operator you son of a bitch!" came crazed words from his lips.

"Jesus!" I told the chopper to give me a run on an azimuth directly behind me, from fifteen meters on out, then I yelled at everybody to lie down.

Then the jungle started disappearing within an arm's reach, as the miniguns decimated the tree line, and the rockets threw wood and dirt and searing metal over our heads. Anybody standing up would have been riddled. We didn't take any fire from that direction.

Then a Green Hornet gunbird appeared out of the ether and hovered directly overhead. The pilot jammed the rudder and spun the chopper in a tight circle right over our heads, while crew chief and door gunner opened up the miniguns. Two horrendous columns of fire erupted from a common center, mowing down the jungle around us, like one of those fireworks that spins in a circle, spewing bright sparks from the center as it spins. Thousands of shiny, hot brass casings rained down upon us, clattering and clinking. It would have been an awe-inspiring sight even if it hadn't been our salvation. The choppers blew the hell out of everything all around us while the slick dropped into the small clearing and we clambered on. I ran to the front of the chopper and stuck my weapon between the pilot and copilot, prepared to fire through their windshield if necessary. Both their helmeted heads turned in my direction, then back to the front, when they saw the hard terror in my face.

The chopper lifted into the sky and we skimmed the trees for a few seconds, gaining airspeed. We poured lead into the jungle until we were at altitude.

The new guy sat against the interior of the chopper with a dazed look on his face. A dud grenade and a jammed rifle on his first mission. I wondered what the odds were on that.

I watched the puffball clouds drop to our level, pondered the action of Fast Eddie down there, saving me from a shot in the back. "Thanks Eddie," I yelled.

Our eyes locked somewhere beyond time. "No problem," he answered.

Chapter 42

Contemplation

Top caught me walking toward the club. "Hey Acre, come here a minute."

"Yeah Top, what can I do for you?" I said.

"Your tour is about up, have you decided if you're going to extend?"

I glanced toward the ground, my eyes fastened on a solitary stem of grass lying flat in the red earth. "No Top, I haven't made up my mind yet."

"Well, here are your papers. They're filled out and ready to go, all you have to do is sign them. I'll have them ready for you if you decide to stay."

"Well thanks, thank you," I nodded.

He looked at me a minute. He wanted me to extend. "OK, go on with whatever you were doing."

I nodded again and headed for the club.

The club was empty and quiet. Aimlessly, I walked to the gate and headed down the road toward town. I pondered the pink buildings at the airfield, never did find out why they were pink, if there was a reason.

I stuck out my thumb toward a jeep heading down the road and caught a ride with a couple of Red Cross girls. Couldn't believe it. Round eyed American girls driving down the highway to Ban Me Thuot.

"Need a lift?"

"You headed for BMT?"

"Sure, hop in."

I climbed in the back of the jeep. Jesus, they had on dresses! The driver was blonde, the other was brunette. From where I was sitting I could see the brunette's suntanned calves.

"You assigned to the B-team in Ban Me Thuot?" the driver asked over her shoulder, blonde curls bouncing. Her eyes met mine momentarily, stayed on the beret a moment, before she looked back to the road.

"No, my unit's back there by the airport."

"What unit is that?"

"CCS, B-50."

"What do you guys do, looks bigger than an A-team?"

"Oh, nothin much."

Before I had a chance to get my bearings we were already in town and they were asking where I was headed. We'd exchanged hardly a dozen words. Having them leave me at the bar felt strange so I let the pock marked buildings go by and asked them to drop me off downtown.

I watched their jeep disappear down the road and muttered to myself, "Round Eyes, real Round Eyes."

Nearby, a couple of cute Vietnamese children were playing in front of some huge clay pots, one little girl wore a bright green silky blouse, which contrasted nicely with the red shirt of the other little girl. They smiled for me while I took their picture.

I walked down the street, watching the bustle of people, feeling like I belonged there, looking in shop windows. The Vietnamese tailor, Mai Son, who had made my walking suit to wear in Bangkok, noticed me standing at the window, looked up from his machine, smiled and waved. The dark Indian stood with arms folded in front of his open shop, its steel gates slid open in the daytime, full of colorful carpets and rugs, brass pots and elephants, wooden statues.

Two women were walking down the sidewalk, window shopping. From a distance they looked familiar. When we were closer I recognized Ling and the Cambode. I was about to speak to them when they saw me approaching. Ling looked startled and lurched around the corner. The Cambode glanced toward me and followed her, talking in Vietnamese.

I rounded the corner and stopped short. Ling stood facing the unpainted wooden alley door. She was crying; the Cambode was speaking sternly to her.

"What's going on?" I asked, "Long time no see."

"Hallo B-50," the Cambode said, nodding, "Ling feel number ten."

"What's the matter Ling?"

The Cambode spoke to her again, softly this time. She turned slowly toward me. Her silk blouse protruded in front, covering her huge abdomen.

"You're going to have a baby Ling!" I said awkwardly.

"You baby," she said sadly.

"My baby? How do you know it's mine?" I said incredulously.

"I know, I know," Ling said slowly and distinctly.

"But, how do you know?" I insisted.

The Cambode interjected, nodding her head forcefully, "She know, you remember first night Rick and you stay all night hotel . . . ."

"Of course I remember," I interrupted, "but I don't see how that makes her certain it is mine."

"You, Ling, your spirit that night," she raised her right hand, the forefinger and the index finger extended, held tightly together. "You make baby!" she said, gesturing emphatically toward me with the two parallel fingers.

"No, no I don't see," I said.

"I know," Ling said again sadly. They turned and walked slowly down the street, leaving me standing bewildered.

I found my perplexed way to the restaurant, sat alone at a small table. White linen tablecloth, cloth napkins, mahogany table, wooden chairs with bamboo seats. Waiter in white shirt and black dress pants brought a menu. Outside, through dusty plate glass, red dirt streets, the bread vendor and her oven at the corner of the block, the old woman selling cane and coal on the sidewalk, a yellow lambretta sped by, veering to give way to an ARVN officer's jeep.

Steak was listed under American Food. I tried it, got a small, well done, piece of meat of unknown origin, a passable attempt at American fries, drank deep black coffee, ordered a whiskey coke, and wondered what to do about Vietnam.

The three o'clock cloudburst came all at once, as usual. The rain poured from the edge of the porch in steady streams, splashing into the mud at the edge of the walk.

A few Americans and Vietnamese were scattered about the tables. I was amused to see the ARVN colonel whose jeep we'd stolen sitting at a table across the room, speaking quietly but forcefully, sounding agitated. His fatigues were starched stiff, he boasted a breast full of medals, wore a bright red scarf. Listening intently to him was a beautiful Vietnamese woman. Her white blouse reflected the ceiling lamps in rainbow shimmers as she brought the chopsticks to her mouth.

"Probably telling her all about the stolen jeep," I thought maliciously.

It brought a smile to think of the day that one of the guys in recon appeared on post with one fine jeep that he stole while this Vietnamese officer was sitting in the restaurant. The next day the Vietnamese colonel appeared at our gate with his entourage and lots of firepower to back him up. His line of vehicles rolled into our compound like a parade. The Vietnamese officer informed our commanding officer that he knew we had his jeep. This display by the sorry bastard pissed off our colonel, and he invited him to inspect all our vehicles and identify his jeep. Of course it was long gone, having been loaded on a blackbird and shipped to our sister unit up north. It was a fine day. We were "all for one and one for all."

Someone bustled through the door, shaking water from his fatigues. It was Top. He headed for my table and sat across from me.

"So what's up Acre?" he asked.

"Just eatin and waitin out the rain," I answered.

Top surveyed the empty plate a moment. "You tired of the mess hall?"

"No," I said truthfully, "just thinking. The mess hall food is good, better than anywhere else I've been in the Army."

The waiter came to the table, Top ordered coffee.

"Trying to make up your mind?"

"Yeah."

He glanced about the room to see if anyone was in earshot, then spoke very quietly, "You know, the HALO stuff is still in the works, similar to what you and Babysan did. If you're interested you can get TDY (temporary duty) to Okinawa for the training." He studied my face.

"What's involved?" I asked.

"I don't want to get into it here, come talk to me if you decide you're interested."

"OK."

"So, how was the food?"

"Fair, it's a long shot from the real thing, kind of Oriental American I guess you could call it."

"I'd like to have a real American hamburger."

"Oh boy, me too, and a real milkshake, boy would I like a milkshake."

He chuckled, downed the rest of his coffee and stood up. "You want a ride back?"

"I think I'll go over to the PX and get a couple of things, thanks anyway."

"PX my ass, you're headed for the bar," he chided.

"No, not today," I shook my head, "not today."

Chapter 43

POW Mission

Crimmings had his fatigue blouse off and was showing us how his horrendously bruised chest was coming along. The spot where the mortar fragment had hit was still a deep blue, with patterns of yellow and blue fanning out all across his chest. It reminded me of a tie-died t-shirt.

"Sergeant Acre, come here a minute." It was Top again, calling from the Recon Head Shed. I slid off the fence where I'd been talking to Crimmings and Rick and headed quickly toward the first sergeant.

"What's up Top?"

"You've got ten days before DEROS (the date I would return to the States)."

"That's right."

"We need a One-One for a POW mission, you've been in Kilo Thirty-six haven't you?" He was studying the After Action Report he held in his hand.

"Kilo Thirty-six was my first mission out of country," I said.

"Well, the place has changed a lot since you were in there. Let's see, you were in there in March, watched a bunch of NVA walk down a trail, stayed around several days, then walked out to Bu Dop."

"Well, we walked back across the river to an LZ," I indicated.

"Yeah, but you stayed in, and then walked out."

"That's right."

"Anyway, like I said, the place has changed, since you guys were in there everybody has been shot out, we've got reports of concrete bunkers, .51 calibers, and 37 millimeter."

"I remember our interpreter said the NVA were complaining about having to build bunkers all day."

"That's what it says here in the After Action Report. You've seen the terrain, and besides, I gave Carly his choice of One-One's and he asked for you. It's a team we're putting together just for this mission. For some reason MACV wants a POW out of here really bad, and if we can't get them a POW I'd like to at least send them some good intel." He cleared his throat, shuffled the papers he was holding. "I'm not going to tell you to run this with ten days left, it's for five days, and the insertion is set for three days from now. If you're in the full five days, that puts you in the field with two days to DEROS, unless you've decided to extend. But, Carly asked for you, so I'm asking you."

"OK, I'll run it Top," I said.

"Good, good, tomorrow morning you'll all meet here and we'll go over this, then they want you at the TOC for the briefing." He turned and opened the battered screen door and went inside.

⊷ ⋈ ⊶

The chopper approached Bu Dop at a higher altitude than usual. The day was clear and dry, the wind rushing through the open door was cooler at this height. Four or five thousand feet below I could see the little compound, the runway looked the length of a postage stamp.

When the chopper was directly above the runway, it suddenly turned on its side and dropped straight down toward the earth. My side of the chopper faced straight down and plummeted in a vertical drop. I sat wide-eyed, my hands gripping the side of the door, watching the runway grow larger and larger in my face as I felt myself falling toward the earth in a sitting position.

After what seemed an eon of falling, and just when it seemed that my face was going to splat into the runway, the chopper righted itself, scooped up the wind on its blades and settled into a perfect landing on the tarmac.

For the first time I looked toward the front of the chopper. Two faces smiling crazily stared back at me from the pilot's and copilot's seats.

"Pretty fancy," I said.

⊷ ⋈ ⊶

As we walked in I strained to see familiar details. It had been too long. But, I did have a feeling for how far it was to the road. After several hours of sneaking slowly, our point man stopped our forward travel. He tiptoed slowly forward, just out of sight, then appeared again in a few minutes. The road was just ahead.

Because we were twelve men instead of the usual six, we had moved even more slowly than usual. It had taken most of the day for us to advance to the road, however we were fairly sure that we had managed to avoid detection.

Carly moved the team about thirty meters from the road, then we inched our way parallel with it, until he found a patch of brambles that was sufficiently dense for us to sit out the night.

After the claymores were set, there was still some light. We poured water into our LRP rations and got ready for an evening meal.

Things were quiet, everyone was intent on getting his dinner ready. The SCU were spaced in a tight circle, with we three Americans, Bill, Carly, and myself, in the center.

"Fuck!" Bill called in a loud whisper. He was looking directly above his head.

Carly and I looked to where he was pointing.

There, two feet directly above our heads, hung a wasps nest. It was nearly dark, too late to move, and the wasps were coming back to their nest for the night.

"What do we do now?" I whispered.

We looked at one another. Bill got that wry smile, and started digging around in his ruck sack.

"What are you thinking?" Carly murmured.

"Just a second," Bill replied quietly. When he brought his hand out of the ruck sack he had his little can of WD-40. He removed the lid carefully. "Let me see your lighter," he whispered.

I handed him my zippo, with some hesitation.

He pointed the can of WD-40 at the wasp nest, lit the cigarette lighter, and pressed the nozzle on the can of oil. A huge flame erupted from the oil can like a miniature flame thrower. He started laughing and couldn't hold the can steady.

The wasps began getting excited.

"Will you get with it?" Carly whispered, choking back his laughter. "Those fuckers are getting pissed."

Finally Bill got the thing aimed and the flame started in the right direction, engulfing the nest in fire. Burning wasps dropped to the ground like miniature fighters on fire. When the flame stopped, the nest was nothing but a small black ember with a meager curl of smoke circling upward.

The light faded into darkness and our thoughts turned to more serious things.

I dozed and awoke throughout the night. I must have fallen somewhat asleep, for Bill poked me into awareness to stand my two hours watch.

The hours passed without incident with only the sounds of the jungle night penetrating the stillness.

When morning came we pulled in the claymores and started moving parallel with the road again to find a suitable place to set up our ambush.

Late in the morning, we stopped near what appeared to be a good place. We were at the base of a large bend in the trail, which had open areas in each direction that could be used as fields of fire. Carly and the point man sneaked up to the trail to get a better look.

Next we heard the sound of an engine coming down the road. Those of us waiting for Carly and the point man looked to one another anxiously. The sound got closer. Carly and the old Montagnard appeared in the foliage just as the sound of the engine seemed very close. They sat down with us. The vehicle downshifted and the motor roared. Closer and closer it came, then brakes squeaked and the vehicle stopped directly opposite where we sat.

It just sat there and idled thirty meters away from us. Each of us looked in the direction of the sound, then we'd look at one another's tense face. We waited. It sat idling.

Finally, the old Montagnard lay down and crawled in the direction of the sound. He was gone only a moment, came crawling back, his lips unmistakably mouthing the word "tank." He drew pictures in the air, pulling his left hand in the air with fingers curled over an imaginary barrel; thirty-seven millimeter guns on the armored vehicle.

Then we started really sweating. We didn't have a LAW (Light Anti-tank Weapon). If it came crashing through the brush toward us, there wasn't much we could do to it. The ground was solid for a long way in the direction of Vietnam. No one had to be reminded that 37mm were hell on choppers.

After what seemed like hours, and after I was sure my heart would burst, the thing revved up, and drove on down the trail.

We sat for some time in silence. Carly sat motionless, immersed in thought.

He finally looked toward Bill and me, moved quietly to where we sat, and whispered, "This place is as good as any. We've got a decent field of fire for the trail security, we've got these trees by the trail, we might as well set up here."

Bill and I nodded our heads. I moved ten or fifteen meters from the trail and sat where Carly motioned that he wanted me. He sent a Yard back with me to help take care of the rear security. The Yard crept into the jungle and set up his claymore, then came back and sat near me.

I got on the radio to make contact with the FAC and give him the code words for setting up an ambush. I remembered my first mission at one-zero school, when Charlie came down the trail before we got set up. For ten or fifteen minutes we would be at our most vulnerable, during the time we were setting up the ambush.

Carly set four men at each end of the bend in the trail, with orders to fire down the trail if anyone approached. He and Bill set up claymores at strategic points along the kill zone of the ambush, and also in the direction of the fields of fire down the trail at each side. He positioned two of the SCU along the ambush kill zone, leaving the other two as trail security.

Then he and Bill positioned themselves in the exact center of the kill zone. At the proper time, the idea was to kill all but one, trying to only wound him. Carly screwed the silencer onto his Swedish K, with which he would try to take a prisoner quietly if possible.

We sat and waited for somebody to come along. A couple of NVA alone hopefully, or maybe just a single soldier, or better yet a couple of nurses, yeah, that would be good, a couple of unarmed nurses that we could run out and grab and nobody would get hurt.

I thought about the story somebody had told me, who was it, about the nurses that got shot along with the NVA when they tried to take prisoners, the ARVNs had run out and grabbed the dead women, dragged them off the trail and started fucking their dead bodies.

But, mostly I was worried. Five days to DEROS, out of the Nam, on the way to the World, or somewhere.

We waited, and waited. I'd learned to sit quietly in awkward positions for hours. I watched the other guys. Everybody was alert to their duties, eyes like hawks peering into the undergrowth, consoled by their own thoughts.

When they did come, how were we to know whether it was two or twenty or two hundred? We didn't, and that was a major problem. You could see down the road a ways, but not far enough to tell whether two or three guys were leading another hundred. The sawed-off RPD machine gun pointed down the trail would be a hell of a deterrent though.

Finally they came, the Yard to the right motioned to the rest of us. Eight of them stretched out a few feet apart, directly in front of us. Carly's weapon was raised, waiting for them to be directly centered in our little ambush. He had his man picked out, Bill and the two SCU were to take the others out since there were more than two.

The bolt on the 9mm Swedish K made an almost noiseless clink, a millisecond later the AK's and Bill's CAR-15 opened up on the other seven. They died without much suffering, though at least three watched themselves die for the last few seconds, lying helpless on the ground, pouring quick rivers of red blood into the earth.

But Carly had picked a heroic one, or perhaps he thought he had been missed, who knows what he thought. At any rate, though he was hit with the 9mm in the right shoulder, he brought his weapon toward us, didn't listen or didn't hear when the interpreter called for him to surrender. They dropped him before he had a chance to open up on us. Our POW was dead.

Carly and Bill ran out to the trail and checked the bodies for papers. I was on the radio, informing FAC of what happened and that we'd be moving out on a given azimuth toward Viet Nam.

We picked up our claymores and hauled ass out of there as quickly as possible.

The FAC pilot set me on a new azimuth and we headed for an LZ. When we reached the opening, I flashed him with my mirror and he affirmed that he had our position and the choppers were on the way.

We could hear the choppers in the distance, the sound of salvation, I was on the horn with the FAC when I heard the unmistakable, unforgettable "ping" in my headset.

"Did you hear that?" I asked the FAC pilot.

"Hear what?" he said.

"I heard a ping."

There was another one, and another.

"Oh, shit affirmative," said the FAC pilot.

Seldom were the guys in the air nervous, they were the ones always calm and cool, helping me find an even track to keep from going out of my mind. This time it was the FAC pilot who was nervous.

The pings got louder and closer together. The radar on Charlie's 37mm was locking in. Soon the pings were less than a second apart.

"We've got to get out of here," the FAC said anxiously.

"I know," I said anxiously. "We'll keep moving east."

The drone of the FAC and the wop wop of the choppers disappeared.

Then came another problem. Somebody was chasing us. We heard people yelling in the direction from which we'd come.

We hauled ass again.

Every few minutes Carly stopped and stuck a claymore or dropped a grenade with a time delay fuse, then we ran like hell. Giving Charlie a little of his own medicine. With explosives going off in front and behind or in the middle of him, he was likely to be shaky about getting too close.

When I got in touch with the FAC again we didn't hear any pinging, but when I was able to flash the plane with the mirror he informed us that we were in the middle of a huge patch of jungle with no LZ's close. Since it was getting late in the afternoon, and we weren't certain we'd lost Charlie, Carly decided to blow an LZ with some claymores.

We soon found an appropriate spot that had trees but limited undergrowth. When the choppers were ten minutes away, we tied claymores to the trees.

When the gunbirds were over us we lay down and blew the claymores at the same time the gunbirds devastated everything around us.

The first slick came in, hovered twenty feet from the ground and dropped the rope ladders. Carly sent six of the SCU scurrying up the ladders.

Climbing a rope ladder in full combat gear up to a hovering chopper is like trying to crawl up spaghetti in a wind storm. All the while wondering if Charlie will pop up and shoot you in the back or if a stray round or piece of shrapnel from the maelstrom going on out there will thump into your body or tear off an appendage.

Hands reached from the chopper door toward me. I let go one hand from the rope and locked wrists with one of them. As the slick picked up its tail and raced toward altitude and safety, helping hands pulled me on board.

Chapter 44

The Hardest Good-bye

It hurt like hell to say it. "I'm not going to extend, what did you decide to do?" I asked.

"I turned in the paperwork while you were in the field," Rick said.

"Yeah? Where you taking leave?"

"Oh," he scratched his head and thought a minute, "I think I'll probably go to Hawaii."

I stood at the window, gazing over the hooches and the bunkers, at some undefined point in the morning sky. "I'd kind of like to stay."

"You ought to, Hawaii would be a blast."

"Have you heard from Steve?"

"He was here a couple of days ago."

"He's got you a job huh?"

"No problem."

"What you going to do?"

He shrugged his shoulders. "Who cares."

"I got the reassignment to Panama that I asked for," I said.

"That's good," he answered halfheartedly.

"Well, anyway, how about if we do a little remodeling in the room here?" I said, trying to lift the mood.

"Sure, what you got in mind?"

"Let's hang some curtains from the walls, just change things around a little."

"OK."

I bought some shiny patterned silk from Mai Son, the tailor in Ban Me Thuot. I stretched wire across the walls and hung the silk from it. Then I put a mat on the floor in place of the mortar crates.

"Let's haul some of this stuff off, this place is getting too full," I suggested.

"I think I can get the half ton," Rick offered.

He returned in fifteen minutes with the truck, and backed it up to the door. We loaded nearly all the furniture we'd scavenged onto the back of the half ton.

We drove off the post and headed toward Ban Me Thuot. It was a clear warm day.

"What should we do with this stuff?" I asked.

"Let's just drive up one of these roads and drop it in the ditch," he answered.

He turned south off the highway when we were several miles from the post, drove a couple of miles, pulled to the side of the road.

"This ought to do it hadn't it?"

"Guess so."

We threw everything out of the back into the bar ditch.

On the way back Rick lit a joint, handed it to me for a toke.

"Deak is gonna shit when he sees the room, think he'll like it?"

"I doe-no," Rick smiled.

———————

I studied the box of tapes we'd made over the months: Mike Bloomfield, Iron Butterfly, Brian Auger and the Trinity, Wes Montgomery, Sailor by the Steve Miller Band, Beatles, Janis Joplin, Chicago, Three Dog Night, Bob Dylan.

"Guess I'll leave you the tapes, is your tape player working OK still?"

"Yeah, it's working fine."

The door opened, in stepped Deak. I looked at him, remembering the day we'd met, so long ago.

This time his mouth dropped open and he gaped at what he saw.

"What did you guys do to the room?" he finally said.

"Did a little redecorating, what do you think, pretty neat huh?"

"Yeah, I guess." He set his ruck down and ran his fingers over the cloth on the walls. "Where did you get this stuff?"

"Bought it at Mai Son's, the best he had."

"Jeez," he said, moving past us and getting a beer from the refrigerator.

Turning toward me he opened his beer and spoke again, "So, you heading for Panama?"

"Got the orders today."

— ◄+► —

I packed all my sterile fatigues in a laundry bag, picked up the little tape player and other odds and ends and headed for the SCU's barracks.

"Bo, here is some stuff for you guys, you take." I set the bag on the floor, handed Bo the tape player.

Bo jabbered something in Chinese, the other SCU who were lounging around in the barracks jumped up and joined us, immediately took the fatigues out of the bag, held them up to themselves to check a possible fit, talking and nodding, saying "Number one!"

"Well, I gotta get my stuff packed," I turned and headed back for my hooch.

"Acre! Get over to the head shed and sign some papers!" Top yelled out the door when I walked by.

"You bet, Top," I said.

S1 and S2 were humming with activity. I reported to the XO, who motioned toward a chair in front of the next desk, then told the captain to take care of me. It was the same captain who had jumped us into the trees on the parachute infiltration.

While the captain went for something in the next room, I noticed the curtain was back so I scrutinized the large map of CCS area of operations. Targets were outlined in grease pencil, with their names written in. Markers were placed where teams were in a given target, other markers noted the location of upcoming arc lights.

The captain returned with a form in his hand.

"You need to sign this form," he said stiffly, laying the paper on the desk.

It stated that I was aware of and agreed, under penalty of law, to reveal nothing about the nature of this mission for ten years, or face a ten thousand dollar fine and ten years in prison.

I read it, signed it, asked the captain if there was anything else.

Avoiding my eye, he said that was all.

— ◄+► —

I packed the things I was sending home. I wrapped my stereo amplifier in the poncho liner that I'd covered up with in the field for the past year, packed the tape player and the speakers, the chess boards from Taipei.

Good-byes were always difficult for me, so I didn't say many. Rick drove me to the airport the next morning. We didn't talk much. Not many words to be spoken.

When the blackbird landed, he drove out onto the tarmac, and pulled up behind the lowered ramp. I grabbed the duffel bag, threw it across my shoulder, shook his hand, walked up the ramp and sat near the rear of the plane. He sat on the back of the truck seat, his faded boonie hat throwing a shadow across his furrowed brow. The ramp slowly raised, just before it closed, he raised his hand. I waved, and he disappeared from view.

Chapter 45

Busy Being Born

Nha Trang was the same, but it looked different, I was seeing through other eyes. I was without my friends, didn't know a soul, and was leaving country instead of coming in country. I hauled my duffel bag and suitcase past the flags, up the steps, and into the Headquarters Building, 5th Special Forces Group, Airborne.

A memorial on the wall caught my eye immediately. I set the luggage down in front of the display and studied it. There was a plaque for every Special Forces soldier killed or missing in action in Vietnam. I found Jim's name, Thomas, Babysan, Jerry, Sergeant Shriver, Jenkins, Mike. I slowly ran my fingers across the engraving of each name, as though it were Braille. My mind and heart spun into the spaces of the past year, drifting through the times I'd known with each of them.

Dimly, far away, at the end of a long dark tunnel, a voice was impinging on my melancholy vision. The tone was loud and insistent.

"Sergeant, sergeant. Sergeant!"

I turned, a lieutenant was speaking to me. I glanced at the yellow bars of a second lieutenant on his shoulder, then slowly gazed at the pale white skin of a face with no suntan, surrounding eyes that had just come to Vietnam.

"Yes sir," I murmured, turning back toward the plaque.

207

"You need to go see the sergeant major," he said.

"See the sergeant major?" I queried.

"You need a hair cut, now get going and see the sergeant major!" he snapped.

"Yes sir," I glared contemptuously at his tailored, starched jungle fatigues.

I stuck my beret into the open end of the duffel bag and headed for the Group sergeant major's office. "Got a fucking second lieutenant policing the halls for hair cuts," I muttered to myself. It was a trip I didn't relish. This sergeant major was the most powerful enlisted man in the Group.

I knocked on the door, a gruff voice said to enter.

"Sergeant Acre reporting Sergeant Major," I said and stood at attention.

He looked up from his desk, broad shoulders held straight, steely gray eyes that contrasted with short gray hair studied every detail of my appearance.

"You need a haircut, go get one now," he finally said.

"I did get one just before I left Ban Me Thuot, Sergeant Major," I braved.

"Good, it's still too long and you're not leaving country without a hair cut and cutting those side burns and trimming that mustache, do I make myself clear?"

"Right Sergeant Major, I'll go get a haircut right now," I agreed.

I left his office and returned to where my duffel bag and suitcase sat beside the memorial plaques. What I found there I could not believe. My beret was not visible in the end of the duffel. Frantically I opened the end of the duffel, maybe I'd stuffed it in further than I remembered. It was gone! Someone had stolen it. My old, first, original, rat nibbled beret had been stolen by some clerk jerk remington raider no good REMF (rear echelon mother fucker)!

I was baffled, frustrated, then furious, but there was nothing to do but break out a new one. The old one had fit so well, the creases just right, had felt so comfortable.

In a veritable ugly mood I picked up my possessions and headed for the barracks to my temporary quarters.

After locking everything in a wall locker I hunted for a phone. I found several phones attached to the side of a building near the air strip, pulled Steve's number out of my wallet and called Saigon.

"Steve, this is Ernie, what you doing?"

"I'm working on some paperwork, where are you?" The phone crackled and popped, Steve's voice sounded as though he were talking into a barrel.

"In Nha Trang."

"What are you doing in Nha Trang?" His voice reminded me vaguely of the reverberators we attached to the AM radios in our cars back in the World.

"I'm headed for Panama, but I want to stay too."

"Well, come on up, just catch a flight to Saigon, we'll straighten out your paperwork when you get here," he said.

"I just don't know what to do Steve."

From the direction of the airstrip I heard several explosions, the ground shook under my feet, black smoke rose from behind some buildings. The wail of a siren echoed throughout the compound.

"What's going on down there, I hear sirens," Steve asked.

"The airfields getting mortared Steve, I'm calling from right beside the airstrip, I better get off the phone and get away from here," I said.

"OK, catch a plane and give me a call from Tan Son Nhut when you get here if you decide to stay."

"OK, thanks a lot, see you." I hung up the phone and hurried back to the barracks across camp.

The stolen beret and the airfield attack I took as a sign and made the decision. I was headed for the World.

I was lounging on a cot with my boots propped on the end of the bedstead, when a familiar voice said, "Acre, you ready to head for Cam Ranh?"

It was the supply sergeant who had been wounded on his solitary mission with me on the arc light.

We shook hands. "I heard you got a job as Liaison, how do you like it?" I asked. I noticed the CIB stitched on his fatigue blouse.

"It's a great job, of course I like Nha Trang. So you're headed for the World, where you going?"

"I'm headed for Panama after I take thirty days at home."

"Well, tell you what, let me give you a lift to Cam Ranh, I've got to deliver some stuff over there, you can ride along with me and take a look at the country."

"Sounds good."

"Tell you what, I'll pick you up here at," he looked at his watch, "1300 hours."

"OK, I'll be here."

I wandered around the compound during the couple of hours remaining, looking at the signs again, the museum, the model of the A Team camp, the .51 caliber, whose white tracers I'd come to know and fear, thinking of that first innocent day when Mike and I had surveyed these things, hoping, wondering if maybe he was alive somewhere, but knowing better.

It really was a beautiful day for a drive and I was glad I took the lift instead of flying. The road was paved and it paralleled a gorgeous ridge of mountains on one side, the blue South China Sea on the other.

The air was cool and felt delicious. The ocean waves rolled rhythmically onto white sandy beaches. Between the road and the mountains, Vietnamese in cone hats tended their rice paddies, further up, water buffalo worked the fields. The paddies were calm, still lakes, the mountains reflected in their waters.

Enjoying the breeze in the open jeep, contemplating the idyllic scene all around, I said, "Boy, this is quite a sight, I never realized it was so pretty between Nha Trang and Cam Ranh."

"Yeah, I always enjoy this drive when it's nice out," the supply sergeant answered.

"The mountains look so peaceful, reaching toward the sky, you'd never know there was a war out there."

The cool breeze on my face, the waves reaching musically toward the road ahead, the shimmering mountains, all these conspired together and my eyelids became heavy.

— ⊯ —

The yellow-disc sun suspended above the mountain burned into my soul and I could see each engraved brass plate back at the memorial shining blindingly bright, and then there were many suns above the gleaming mountains.

I noticed a group of soldiers in the distance, they were standing in a circle, watching something on the ground.

"See those guys up there?" I said.

"Up where?" he looked in the direction I was pointing.

"Way up on the edge of that rise, just below the many suns, right next to where the jungle stops."

He slowed the jeep and pulled to the edge of the road. "You mean that bunch of guys off in the distance? Hell, you can barely see them."

"Yeah, but what are they looking at on the ground?"

"Well, let's go see," he whipped the jeep around and headed up a trail that led toward their location.

After a few minutes of bumping over the rough track, we could clearly see the group of soldiers.

"Looks like a recon team, there's only what, eight of them?" the supply sergeant said.

"Probably, look at what they've got there!" I exclaimed.

"Geez, look at the size of that thing! It must be twenty feet long," he said.

It was a huge grey python, lying lifeless in their midst.

"Look how big around it is, that guy is sitting on it, he's got his rifle leaning up against it."

"That is the biggest snake I have ever seen."

"You know what?" I said.

"What?"

"That guy sitting on the snake. He looks just like Babysan, I mean, that could be Babysan! See how little he is, look at that baby face, that fuzzy red mustache."

The guy sitting on the snake waved to us. We waved back.

"Quite a catch you guys got there!"

"Yeah, scared us to death," the man sitting on the snake answered. His face was smirking but his eyes betrayed a haunted loneliness.

"See you." We waved again as the supply sergeant turned the jeep and headed back down the path toward the road.

"Sure glad I never ran into one of those, I was always more afraid of running into a cobra," I said. I recalled the times leaning against a tree in the blackness of night, wondering if the story was true about the cobra making every widening circles around its nest of newborn, killing everything within a given radius.

"I didn't know there were any recon teams like ours around here," the supply sergeant mused.

"Like ours?" I asked.

"Yeah, those Yards had NVA fatigues and AK's, didn't you notice?"

"Hell I didn't give it a second thought, just looked normal to me, but you're right," I answered.

I turned to look over my shoulder. "Hey, they're gone!"

"What?" He stopped the jeep. "Where in the hell? They couldn't have carried that snake away could they?"

"Beats the shit out of me."

⊷⊶⊶⊶⊶

"Hey, wake up, you're missing the scenery, looking at the floor board like that," the supply sergeant said. "You awake?"

"Yeah, you're right," I forced my eyes open and my thoughts back to reality.

"So what were you so engrossed in?"

"Oh nothin, I was just thinking about a dream I had a long time ago," adding quietly, as though it was an afterthought, "almost exactly a year ago as a matter of fact."

"A dream?"

"Yeah, I dreamed there was a black snake coiled up on my chest, no big deal."

Glossary

Airborne – Qualified to make static line parachute jumps.

AO – Area of operations.

Arc Light – B-52 bombardment.

B-40 – See RPG.

Beau Coup Number Ten – Extremely bad.

Beau Coup – Very, extremely, or many.

Blackbird – SOG's transport planes, C-123 and C-130 military transports, painted black, without any markings.

BMT – Ban Me Thuot.

C&C man – Man who ran recon for SOG.

C&C – Command and Control.

C-4 – Plastic explosive. Looks similar to Playdough, can be molded and formed.

CAR-15 – M-16 rifle with a short barrel and collapsible sliding stock, defined as a submachine gun.

CCC – Command and Control Central.

CCN – Command and Control North.

CCS – Command and Control South.

Charlie – The enemy.

Chopper – Helicopter.

CIB – Combat Infantryman's Badge, awarded for being in combat.

Claymore or Claymore Mine – Highly effective, command detonated, antipersonnel mine, set out around the perimeter of a recon team's nighttime position. Also used in many other applications by all combat arms. Could be time or trip detonated with the proper fuses. Fleeing recon teams left Claymores and grenades with time delay fuses in the path of pursuers. When C-4 was not available, the Claymore could be taken apart and the C-4 inside could be used for other applications, even lighted and used to heat a cup of coffee, not in the field of course.

Concertina – Rolled wire with sharp barbs or razors, used to protect the perimeter of military camps.

CS and CS Grenade – Tear gas in a powder form, carried by recon teams. The powder was used to dust the trail behind a team to discourage dogs. The grenades were dropped behind a fleeing team to discourage pursuit.

Dinky dau – Crazy.

DZ – Drop zone, clearing for a parachutist to land.

Escape and Evasion – In recon, term used to define a pre-determined plan and route of escape should communications fail, a team member be separated from the team, or any other of a multitude of disasters strike.

FAC – Forward Air Control.

Field of Fire – Area open and within effective range of a weapon.

Firefight – Engaged in exchange of fire with the enemy, used when the recon team was unable to flee or disengage the enemy and had to stay in place and fight in a defensive stance.

FNG – Fucking New Guy.

Fuck – All around descriptive word, a noun, verb, adjective, or adverb depending on usage.

Garrison – Duty at or near a military headquarters, as opposed to field duty.

Green Hornet – Amphetamine issued to and carried by recon teams for emergency use.

Green Hornets – Air Force 20th Special Operations Squadron, which supported CCS recon teams. Highly respected by CCS recon people.

Gunbird – Huey helicopter outfitted as an offensive support weapon, with rockets and miniguns.

HAHO – High Altitude High Opening parachute jumping, minimum free falling, maximum time with the parachute deployed, can be used to traverse long distances before reaching the ground.

HALO – High Altitude Low Opening parachute jumping; free falling before deploying the parachute.

HE – High explosive.

Illumination Round – Projectile usually fired from a mortar that lights up the field of fire at night by burning phosphorus, held aloft by a small parachute.

KIA – Killed in Action.

KP – Kitchen Police, i.e. assigned to work in the kitchen.

Lifer – Extremely pejorative term for a career military person, as opposed to soldier or professional soldier.

LZ – Landing zone.

MACV-SOG – Military Assistance Command Vietnam – Studies and Observations Group. The innocuous sounding name Studies and Observations Group was used instead of Special Operations Group.

MIA – Missing in Action.

Mini-gun – Modern version of the Gattling gun, a multibarreled 7.62mm machine gun, the set of barrels being rotated rapidly by an electric motor, allowing for extremely high cyclic rate of fire while minimizing overheating of gun barrels.

Mortar and Mortar Tube – High trajectory close support weapon, fired by dropping a projectile inside a large tube which sits at a steep angle.

Nha Trang – coastal city in southern South Vietnam.

Number One – Good or very good.

Number Ten – Bad or very bad, see beau coup number ten.

Nung – Vietnamese who were ethnic Chinese. Fine soldiers.

NVA – North Vietnamese Army , the Regular Army of North Vietnam.

One-One – Recon team number two man, usually the radio operator.

One-Two – Third man on a recon team, usually the newest man on the team.

One-Zero – Recon team leader.

Panel – Orange plastic sheet about a foot square, used as a signaling device by recon teams.

Perimeter – the outside limits of a military compound.

POW – Prisoner of War.

Project Omega – Detachment B-50, CCS's predecessor at Ban Me Thuot, before the assets were transferred to MACV-SOG. CCS was also known as Project Omega and as B-50 during my tour of duty.

Recon – Reconnaissance.

REMF – Rear echelon mother-fucker.

Remington Raider – Pejorative term for a clerk or other REMF.

RPD – Russian machine gun.

RPG – B-40 "Rocket Propelled Grenade" A misnomer, the bulbous projectile carrying a shaped charge was expelled from the shoulder fired tube by a black powder charge. Russian and Chinese.

SCU – Acronym for Special Commando Unit, pronounced "Sioux," we used it to refer to our indigenous team members.

SFC – Sergeant First Class.

Shaped Charge – An explosive charge designed so that the force of the explosion is directional.

Slick – Huey helicopter used to transport troops, as opposed to a gunbird.

SOI – Signal Operator's Instructions.

SOP – Standard Operating Procedure.

Static line – The line which is attached to the airplane or helicopter and which pulls out the parachute from the bag on the jumper's back.

Sterile – Free of any tags or markings that could indicate U.S. origins.

TOC – Tactical Operations Center. At CCS, command center of the unit.

VC – Viet Cong.

Viet Cong – South Vietnamese guerrilla fighters who supported the North.

VR – Visual Reconnaissance. At CCS referred to the fly-over of the target prior to a mission in order to pick out primary and secondary landing zones.

WIA – Wounded in Action.

Willie-Peter – White phosphorous.

XO – Executive Officer, the Commanding Officer's right hand man.

Yard – Slang for Montagnard tribesmen, beloved by Special Forces.

WELCOME TO

Hellgate Press

Hellgate Press is named after the historic and rugged Hellgate Canyon on southern Oregon's scenic Rogue River. The raging river that flows below the canyon's towering jagged cliffs has always attracted a special sort of individual — someone who seeks adventure. From the pioneers who bravely pursued the lush valleys beyond, to the anglers and rafters who take on its roaring challenges today — Hellgate Press publishes books that personify this adventurous spirit. Our books are about military history, adventure travel, and outdoor recreation. On the following pages, we would like to introduce you to some of our latest titles and encourage you to join in the celebration of this unique spirit.

Our books are in your favorite bookstore or you can order them direct at *1-800-228-2275 or visit our Website at http://www.psi-research.com/hellgate.htm*

ARMY MUSEUMS
West of the Mississippi   ISBN: 1-55571-395-5
by Fred L. Bell, SFC Retired   Paperback: 17.95

A guide book for travelers to the army museums of the west, as well as a source of information about the history of the site where the museum is located. Contains detailed information about the contents of the museum and interesting information about famous soldiers stationed at the location or specific events associated with the facility. These twenty-three museums are in forts and military reservations which represent the colorful heritage in the settling of the American West.

BYRON'S WAR
I Never Will Be Young Again...   ISBN: 1-55571-402-1
by Byron Lane   Hardcover: 21.95

Based on letters that were mailed home and a personal journal written more than fifty years ago during World War II, Byron's War brings the war life through the eyes of a very young air crew officer. It depicts how the life of this young American changed through cadet training, the experiences as a crew member flying across the North Atlantic under wartime hazards to the awesome responsibility assigned to a nineteen year-old when leading hundreds of men and aircraft where success or failure could seriously impact the outcome of the war.

GULF WAR DEBRIEFING BOOK

An After Action Report ISBN: 1-55571-396-3
by Andrew Leyden Paperback: 18.95

Whereas most books on the Persian Gulf War tell an "inside story" based on someone else's opinion, this book lets you draw your own conclusions about the war by providing you with a meticulous review of events and documentation all at your fingertips. Includes lists of all military units deployed, a detailed account of the primary weapons used during the war, and a look at the people and politics behind the military maneuvering.

FROM HIROSHIMA WITH LOVE

ISBN: 1-55571-404-8
by Raymond A. Higgins Paperback: 18.95

This remarkable story is written from actual detailed notes and diary entries kept by Lieutenant Commander Wallace Higgins. Because of his industrial experience back in the United States and with the reserve commission in the Navy, he was an excellent choice for military governor of Hiroshima. Higgins was responsible for helping rebuild a ravaged nation of war. He developed an unforeseen respect for the Japanese, the culture, and one special woman.

NIGHT LANDING

A Short History of West Coast Smuggling ISBN: 1-55571-449-8
by David W. Heron Paperback: 13.95

Night Landing reveals the true stories of smuggling off the shores of California from the early 1800s to the present. It is a provocative account of the many attempts to illegally trade items such as freon, drugs, sea otters, and diamonds. This unusual chronicle also profiles each of these ingenious, but over-optimistic criminals and their eventual apprehension.

ORDER OF BATTLE

Allied Ground Forces of Operation Desert Storm ISBN: 1-55571-493-5
by Thomas D. Dinackus Paperback: 17.95

Based on extensive research, and containing information not previously available to the public, *Order of Battle: Allied Ground Forces of Operation Desert Storm*, is a detailed study of the Allied ground combat units that served in Operation Desert Storm. In addition to showing unit assignments, it includes the insignia and equipment used by the various units in one of the largest military operations since the end of WWII.

PILOTS, MAN YOUR PLANES!

A History of Naval Aviation ISBN: 1-55571- 466-8
by Wilbur H. Morrison Hardbound: 33.95

An account of naval aviation from Kitty Hawk to the Gulf War, *Pilots, Man Your Planes!* tells the story of naval air growth from a time when planes were launched from battleships to the major strategic element of naval warfare it is today. Full of detailed maps and photographs. Great for anyone with an interest in aviation.

REBIRTH OF FREEDOM

From Nazis and Communists to a New Life in America ISBN: 1-55571-492-7
by Michael Sumichrast   Paperback: 16.95

"...a fascinating account of how the skill, ingenuity and work ethics of an individual, when freed from the yoke of tyranny and oppression, can make a lasting contribution to Western society. Michael Sumichrast's autobiography tells of his first loss of freedom to the Nazis, only to have his native country subjected to the tyranny of the Communists. He shares his experiences of life in a manner that makes us Americans, and others, thankful to live in a country where individual freedom is protected."

— *General Alexander M. Haig, Former Secretary of State*

THE WAR THAT WOULD NOT END

U.S. Marines in Vietnam, 1971-1973   ISBN: 1-55571-420-X
by Major Charles D. Melson, USMC (Ret)   Paperback: 19.95

When South Vietnamese troops proved unable to "take over" the war from their American counterparts, the Marines had to resume responsibility. Covering the period 1971-1973, Major Charles D. Melson, who served in Vietnam, describes all the strategies, battles, and units that broke a huge 1972 enemy offensive. The book contains a detailed look at this often ignored period of America's longest war.

WORDS OF WAR

From Antiquity to Modern Times   ISBN: 1-55571-491-9
by Gerald Weland   Paperback: 13.95

Words of War is a delightful romp through military history. Lively writing leads the reader to an under- standing of a number of soldierly quotes. The result of years of haunting dusty dungeons in libraries, obscure journals and microfilm files, this unique approach promises to inspire many casual readers to delve further into the circumstances surrounding the birth of many quoted words.

WORLD TRAVEL GUIDE

A Resource for Travel and Information   ISBN: 1-55571- 494-3
by Barry Mowell   Paperback: 19.95

The resource for the modern traveler, *World Travel Guide: A Resource for Travel and Information* is both informative and enlightening. It contains maps, social and economic information, concise information concerning entry requirements, availability of healthcare, transportation and crime. Numerous Website and embassy listings are provided for additional free information. A one-page summary contains general references to the history, culture and other characteristics of interest to the traveler or those needing a reference atlas.

TO ORDER OR FOR MORE INFORMATION
CALL 1-800-228-2275

K-9 SOLDIERS

Vietnam and After
by Paul B. Morgan

ISBN: 1-55571-495-1
Paperback: 13.95

A retired US Army officer, former Green Beret, Customs K-9 and Security Specialist, Paul B. Morgan has written *K-9 Soldiers*. In his book, Morgan relates twenty-four brave stories from his lifetime of working with man's best friend in combat and on the streets. They are the stories of dogs and their handlers who work behind the scenes when a disaster strikes, a child is lost or some bad guy tries to outrun the cops.

AFTER THE STORM

A Vietnam Veteran's Reflection
by Paul Drew

ISBN: 1-55571-500-1
Paperback: 14.95

Even after twenty-five years, the scars of the Vietnam War are still felt by those who were involved. *After the Storm: A Vietnam Veteran's Reflection* is more than a war story. Although it contains episodes of combat, it does not dwell on them. It concerns itself more on the mood of the nation during the war years, and covers the author's intellectual and psychological evolution as he questions the political and military decisions that resulted in nearly 60,000 American deaths.

GREEN HELL

The Battle for Guadalcanal
by William J. Owens

ISBN: 1-55571-498-6
Paperback: 18.95

This is the story of thousands of Melanesian, Australian, New Zealand, Japanese, and American men who fought for a poor insignificant island is a faraway corner of the South Pacific Ocean. For the men who participated, the real battle was of man against jungle. This is the account of land, sea and air units covering the entire six-month battle. Stories of ordinary privates and seamen, admirals and generals who survive to claim the victory that was the turning point of the Pacific War.

OH, WHAT A LOVELY WAR

A Soldier's Memoir
by Stanley Swift

ISBN: 1-55571-502-8
Paperback: 14.95

This book tells you what history books do not. It is war with a human face. It is the unforgettable memoir of British soldier Gunner Stanley Swift through five years of war. Intensely personal and moving, it documents the innermost thoughts and feelings of a young man as he moves from civilian to battle-hardened warrior under the duress of fire.

THROUGH MY EYES

91st Infantry Division, Italian Campaign 1942-1945   ISBN: 1-55571-497-8
by Leon Weckstein
Paperback: 14.95

Through My Eyes is the true account of an Average Joe's infantry days before, during and shortly after the furiously fought battle for Italy. The author's front row seat allows him to report the shocking account of casualties and the rest-time shenanigans during the six weeks of the occupation of the city of Trieste. He also recounts in detail his personal roll in saving the historic Leaning Tower of Pisa.